THE TRUTH ABOUT
THE PILGRIMS

ANO·DON·1657
ÆTIS·SVÆ·5

COPYRIGHT A. S. BURBANK. PLYMOUTH. MASS.

Photographs courtesy Pilgrim Society

GOV. EDWARD WINSLOW

THE TRUTH ABOUT
THE PILGRIMS

By

Francis R. Stoddard

CLEARFIELD COMPANY

Originally Published by the
Society of Mayflower Descendants
in the State of New York
New York, 1952

Reprinted with Corrections
by permission of the
General Society
of Mayflower Descendants
Genealogical Publishing Co., Inc.
Baltimore, 1973

Baltimore, 1976

Library of Congress Catalogue Card Number 73-7218
International Standard Book Number 0-8063-0561-4

Reprinted for
Clearfield Company, Inc. by
Genealogical Publishing Co., Inc.
Baltimore, Maryland
1992, 1993, 1995

Made in the United States of America

CONTENTS

PREFACE

The author of THE TRUTH ABOUT THE PIL-
GRIMS, Colonel Francis R. Stoddard, is a graduate of
Harvard University and a member of the New York bar.
He served in the Spanish-American War, on the Mexican
border, and in World War I. During World War II, he was
for over three years military aide to Mayor La Guardia of
New York City. He has written several books on genealogy
and history, and many articles on insurance in which he
has specialized as a lawyer.

He has served both as Governor General of the General
Society of Mayflower Descendants and as Governor General
of the General Society of Colonial Wars.

His father was descended from ten passengers on the
"Mayflower," and was born in Plymouth. All of his life
Colonel Stoddard has been interested in Pilgrim history.
He is considered an outstanding authority on Pilgrim and
Colonial history.

Many books have been written concerning the Pilgrims,
but few, if any, about their social background and cir-
cumstances.

Colonel Stoddard has spent several years in research on
this book. It answers questions about all the passengers and
the known members of the crew who came to America on
the "Mayflower" in 1620. It also contains what is probably
the best bibliography on the subject ever published.

Writing this book has been a labor of love. The author
has made a sacrifice of time and energy in order to give
students of our early history and the libraries of this country an authoritative book that otherwise would never have
been published.

WALTER M. PRATT
Governor General of the General
Society of Mayflower Descendants

INTRODUCTION

Until recent times, the histories written concerning the Pilgrims have been published with the idea of adding to the general knowledge of them. The writers may have been led into some inaccuracies, but these were few and unintentional. These writers tried conscientiously to give an honest and true picture of the Pilgrims.

Recently there has arrived the debunking accounts of our Country's heroes, written generally by people with leftist leanings and without any regard for undistorted truth. These books have been written *to sell,* and unfortunately several have become "best sellers." No outstanding personage in our Country's history has been safe. The founders of this Country have been especially attacked. There seems to have been a deliberate attempt to falsify history and to misrepresent early ideals and deeds.

It seems easy to write a "best seller" if one does not "let the truth spoil a good story." If one shows the Pilgrims as they were, he runs the danger of being accused of "gilding the lily" and not making them human. If one deliberately misrepresents by intimating that the Pilgrims never saw Plymouth Rock, that they came from the scum of England, that they were bigots who persecuted all who disagreed with them, that they oppressed the Indians, that they were Communists, that they brought no institutions to these shores of any value, that the Compact signed in the cabin of the "Mayflower" was of no importance, and then dresses up these palpable untruths in clever and fine language, one may have a "best seller." Incidentally all of the foregoing mis-statements have appeared in print.

It is interesting to know where many of the misrepresentations originated. Unfortunately many were originated and perpetuated by the descendants of the Pilgrims and by their sincere friends. The libel that Mrs. Dorothy (May) Bradford committed suicide was invented by a fiction writer, who was a Mayflower descendant. The statement that the More children came from a London poorhouse was invented by one of the best friends the Pilgrims ever had. He stated as fact a theory, to explain their presence on the "Mayflower." This theory was later found to be quite erroneous, yet once invented, the error persists. The statement that Richard More changed his name to Mann and went to live in Scituate was invented by a very well intentioned town historian. The discredited fallacy that John Tilley married Bridget van der Velde was originated when a sincere friend mistakenly believed the Dutch record referred to Pilgrim John. The statement that all of the Pilgrims came of yeoman stock, when really some of them held the status of gentlemen, has been repeated by sincere historians who failed to realize the danger of stating generalities. The worst libel concerning the so-called "servants" or employees on the "Mayflower" is to call them "indentured servants," which was the lowest form of service. There is no proof that any of them were indentured. How can one condemn the author of a Pilgrim best seller for giving a lurid picture of the "indentured" slaves who came on the "Mayflower" when their descendants continue to make the mis-statement?

I have read so many untruths concerning the Pilgrims that I have tried to set forth in this volume the truth about them. I have also tried to furnish authorities for all statements made. The book represents an honest attempt to depict truthfully one of the most remarkable groups of persons in our Country's history. They lived in stern times, and yet in the face of what seemed to be unsurmountable obstacles, they devoted themselves to their ideals and were willing to give their property and lives for conscience sake. They placed their trust in God and "accomplished the impossible."

The Pilgrims are not here to answer the untruths spread concerning them. It is the duty of those who revere this country and its founders to protect their memories. I hope that this book will aid in showing what are the real facts concerning them and that it will be a source of enjoyment to all who are interested in knowing the truth about the Pilgrims.

In closing I desire to thank those who have gone over my manuscript and have made possible the publication of this book. Among those many persons, I should especially mention Meredith B. Colket, Jr., and John C. Pearson who made valuable suggestions. Leon C. Hills favored me with his advice. Colonel Walter Merriam Pratt, the distinguished Governor-General of the General Society of Mayflower Descendants, has always been an inspiration. Secretary-General Walter Lester Glenney has helped much.

I appreciate especially the able efforts of the New York Committee led by William J. Meeneghan, Governor Shelby Collom Davis, former Governor Warren Prosser Smith, and Mrs. Rolf T. Michelsen. Mr. Meeneghan has taken complete charge of the physical effort necessary to publish this work. He deserves the thanks of all who have desired to have this book published. Harry B. Sherman has been of great help.

Last but not least, I am grateful to Mrs. A. P. Kelly for giving her valuable time in typing the manuscript. Others too numerous to mention have helped me, and I thank them all.

Francis R. Stoddard

June 1951
New York City

The Truth about the Pilgrims

AN OUTSTANDING event in the history of the United States was the coming from England to America of the "Mayflower" with its small band of Pilgrims. Their fame has extended to every land. Their descendants may justly be proud of being descended from this most remarkable group. All Americans have cause to be proud of the Pilgrims; every American owes them a debt of gratitude.

Why are the Pilgrims outstanding? Why have they left a heritage to America that will never be forgotten? What deeds were performed by this harassed group of men and women which leave Americans forever in their debt? In this account I shall give details of the lives of these people "whose unselfish loyalty to great principles of religion and liberty were destined to make them famous to coming generations." *(BR V)*. I shall try to describe herein what has brought to the Pilgrims the admiration of succeeding generations of Americans.

The giving of the Bible to the mass of the English people convinced them that the Medieval Christian Church had strayed from the practices and doctrines of Christ. They found that religious forms and beliefs adopted from pagan religions or instituted by clerics to strengthen the political structure of the church had taken the place of the simple teachings of Christ. England was largely controlled by an oppressive clergy. Its lands were largely owned by the Church which did everything to increase its holdings. Persons daring to oppose the clergy were often burned alive or tortured with barbarous punishments.

1

Notwithstanding threatened death, mutilation, imprisonment and loss of all property by confiscation, fearless men and women led by John Wickliffe and later reformers laid the foundations of the Reformation which extended gradually all over England. They maintained the authority of scripture as the supreme arbiter of all things in the Church. They sought after that which was eternal as opposed to that which was merely of human ordinance. They made nought of pilgrimages, penances and oblations in comparison with holiness and charity. Their inspiration came from returning to the original faith. *(BR 18-19)*. Because they protested against the abuses of the existing Church, they were known as Protestants. The Act of 1401 for the burning of heretics was powerless to shake the convictions of earnest persons *(BR 20)*. The history of England during the Middle Ages is largely an account of a chronic conflict between the English State, composed of King and Parliament, and the Church which was governed from Rome. Henry VIII did not lead in the break with Rome which resulted in the Act of Supremacy passed in 1534. A great mass of the English people had long clamored for freedom from foreign clerical oppression, and the King followed the desires of a large number of his subjects when he declared in that year the English Church independent. Thereafter, the Bible, translated into English by William Tyndale a few years previously, was read openly by the people instead of being read by stealth as a prohibited book. The service book used in the Churches was in English instead of Latin as formerly.

Henry VIII was succeeded by the boy King Edward VI in 1547. When Mary became queen in 1553, she attempted to make England Roman Catholic by force. She only succeeded in making it more Protestant. Hooper, Ridley, Latimer and Cranmer, men of the highest character and leaders of the Protestant movement, were burned alive at the stake. Dexter in "The England and Holland of the

Pilgrims" says, "The high water mark of this frenzied hatred toward all who were not Papists is indicated by a proclamation five months before Mary's death by which comforting, speaking to, touching or even approaching heretics on their way to execution was made punishable by death." Before Mary died in 1558, three hundred persons from all walks of life are said to have been burned alive because of their refusal to change their religion. For example, Bradford in his "Dialogues" tells of the church of which John Rough was pastor and Cuthbert Symson was deacon. An informer testified that they met to read the Bible and to listen to preaching, and that they also collected money to help those of them who were in prison as well as their poor. John Rough was sent to Newgate and ten days later was burned at Smithfield. Symson, after being repeatedly tortured on the rack to make him betray the names of the other members of the congregation but without success, was also burned at Smithfield. Until Mary's death those of the congregation who survived continued to worship secretly (BR 24).

Under Queen Elizabeth there took place the establishment of the Anglican Church, which claimed its descent through the early English missionaries from the original Christian Church, but which denied that the Papacy, allegedly created centuries after Christ, had any right to control their church. The Pope declared Elizabeth excommunicated and deposed and absolved her subjects from all allegiance to her. Dexter says that the intention of Philip II "to send a great fleet to conquer England had been proclaimed openly, while seminary priests and Jesuits were known to be plotting perpetually to kill Elizabeth. The recent assassination of William the Silent had emphasized the dangers of the situation to the English people." In Fulop-Miller's "The Power and Secret of the Jesuits" is described the efforts of Jesuit priests who entered the country by stealth to incite the English people against their government. They forbade Catholics to take an oath of allegiance to their sovereign and did all they could to stir up a rebellion. The answer of the English people was to hunt down and hang the plotters when they could be caught. In 1588, the Spanish Armada sailed to conquer England and to force it to return to Catholicism. It was said that arrangements had been made by those on the fleet to institute the Inquisition as soon as England should be conquered, and that implements of torture had been brought to make the heretics repent. English sailors defeated the Armada, and English Protestantism was saved.

THE PURITANS

Under Elizabeth there began the split in the English Church which gave rise to the Puritan movement. The Puritans demanded a more thorough reformation which should carry the English Church back to the original purity portrayed by the Scriptures. They did not intend to secede or separate from the English Church. They wished to work out their reforms from within the Church. Puritanism first appeared in the form of a protest against certain ceremonies and vestments which were required by law in the celebration of public worship and which the Puritans regarded as symbols of superstition. Soon many of the educated and best people in England joined the movement. The Puritans retained the bishops and archbishops and the structure of the English Church but tried to conform it to what they believed Christ would have desired.

THE SEPARATISTS

The Puritans did not go far enough to satisfy others of the English people who claimed that Christ's Church under the Apostles had been composed of many gatherings of Christians who had no bishops or archbishops and whose leaders obtained their authority from the members of the congregation and not from higher authority. This has given the name Congregationalism to this form of belief. These people determined to abandon the English Church and to form groups, which would worship Christ simply and without form as did the early Christians. Their Church was to be a society of Christian disciples, voluntarily agreeing to govern themselves by the law of Christ as given in the Scriptures. They determined to form groups of worshippers throughout England by the same right by which Churches were first instituted at Jerusalem, Antioch, Corinth, Alexandria, Rome and other places by the early Christians. These persons were called Separatists and were quite different from the Puritans who never seceded from the Church of England *(G 11-13) (Y 414)*.

Persons who joined the Separatist Congregations soon knew that imprisonment, confiscation of property, mutilation and even death might be their fate. Leonard Bacon in "The Genesis of the New England Churches" tells how their leaders, John Copping, Elias Thacker, Henry Barrowe, John Greenwood and John Penry, men of the highest learning and character, were executed. Officers of the law broke into the houses of the Separatists at all hours of the day and night, searching for unlawful books and dragging the Separatists away to prison where they often remained for years without trials. Old people, men and women of all ages with their children, guilty only of worshipping God according to their own consciences, were placed in loathsome dungeons where many died of the jail fever common at that time in the English prisons. Some had their tongues pierced or were burned with hot irons. Persecution might break their bodies but not their spirits.

I shall not take the time to tell about the Separatist Congregation which met at Scrooby. The arrest and imprisonment of most of its members, their release and gradual flight to Holland, their residence in Amsterdam and Leyden, and their coming to America in the "Mayflower" as Pilgrims are a part of our Country's history.

Fortunately there have been left several accounts written by them which tell of them and their experiences. Bradford's "History" is an absorbing account which sets forth their ideals and describes at length their efforts to overcome all obstacles. The correspondence of the Pilgrims and of their friends gives us much information. Mourt's "Relation" gives a very interesting account of their early adventures. Winslow's writings are most helpful. The Records of the First Church in Plymouth tell the Pilgrim's story, much of it based on Bradford's account. Nathaniel Morton's "New England Memorial" was written by one who lived among them and was in a position to learn the facts at first hand. Anyone can get accurate information concerning the lives of the Pilgrims from their own recorded accounts.

BRADFORD'S HISTORY

Governor William Bradford's "History" is one of the most absorbing and outstanding books in American literature. It furnishes full information concerning the Pilgrims and their movements. Its accuracy has been supported by other information which has become available concerning the events described therein.

Its career is interesting. Samuel Bradford made an attestation, attached to it, dated March 20, 1705, which shows that the Governor gave it to his son Deputy Governor William Bradford, who in turn gave it to his son Major John Bradford, the father of Samuel. There is also a memorandum dated June 4, 1728, in which the Rev. Thomas Prince states that he borowed it from Major John Bradford and thereafter deposited it in the New England Library in the tower of the Old South Church in Boston. It was used by several historians including Governor Hutchinson, who may have taken it with him when he precipitately departed for England during the events leading to the Revolution, or it might have been taken by British troops who later occupied the church. It eventually reached the library of the Bishop of London where it remained unnoticed for a long time. In 1844, Bishop Samuel Wilberforce of Oxford published a history of the Protestant Episcopal Church in America, and he referred therein to a manuscript history of Plymouth Colony. American readers guessed at its identity, and in 1855 a copy was received in America through their efforts and was published in the Collections of 1856 of the Massachusetts Historical Society.

The original manuscript remained in the Fulham Library of the Bishop until 1897 when it was presented to the State of Massachusetts and has since reposed in the Massachusetts State Library *(B 15-16)*. These events are ably described by Justin Winsor in "Proceedings of the Massachusetts Historical Society," Volume XIX, pages 106-122.

THE COMPACT

Learning the lesson of toleration from the Dutch in Holland, the Pilgrims brought to these shores many of the institutions which have been the foundation of our government. In the cabin of the "Mayflower" was signed the Compact which is the first document in history to give manhood suffrage to all persons. (See Appendix B). It is one of the most outstanding documents in American history *(M.D. I, 77) (M.D. XXIII, 1, 32) (M.D. XXIV, 49)*. President Charles W. Eliot of Harvard stated his opinion of the Compact at the dedication of the Pilgrim Monument at Provincetown on August 5, 1910, as follows: "From the Compact was to spring not only a stable government for the little colony, but a great series of Constitutions for free states. They started on this continent the practice of electing, by manhood suffrage, the head of a state, for a limited period. It was a small beginning, but who can comprehend or describe the immensity of the outcome?" President Calvin Coolidge has said: "The Pilgrims, the humble of the

7

earth, sailed up out of the infinite, destined to free mankind. On their abiding faith has been reared a Nation, magnificent, beyond their dreams of Paradise. No like body has ever cast so great an influence on human history."

The Compact was signed on board the "Mayflower" on November 21, 1620 (November 11, old style). Bradford's "History" does not give the names of those who signed the original document. The earliest known list of the signers is that contained in Nathaniel Morton's "New England Memorial" published in 1669 *(M.D. I, 77) (M 26) (M.D. XXIII, 1, 32) (M.D. XXIV, 49)*. What happened to the original document is unknown.

OTHER INSTITUTIONS

The Pilgrims began many other of our institutions. They taught and practiced the separation of Church and State as practiced by the Dutch *(M.D. IV, 4)*. They claimed that not merely the clergy but the laity were an integral part of the Church *(M.D. IV, 8)*. They laid stress upon character as the supreme requisite in true religion *(M.D. IV, 9)*. Freedom of religious worship, as practiced by the Dutch, was not the least of the gifts of the Pilgrims who never persecuted anyone on the grounds of his religion. According to Winslow, "Church of England people and Baptist dwelt continuously in Plymouth in peace, except such as openly sought to overturn the Independent Churches. Visitors of all beliefs and no belief were entertained." The French Jesuit Druillette, who came to Boston in 1650, spent a day or two at Plymouth. He especially mentions Bradford's kindness, and the fact that one day being Friday, the Governor gave him an excellent dinner of fish *(R 196-197)*. At the Lord's table the Pilgrims communed with pious Episcopalians, with Calvinists of the French and Dutch Churches and with Presbyterians, and recognized the spiritual fraternity of all who held the faith *(M.D. IV 12-13)*.

As Senator Hoar has said, "Their good senses kept them free from witchcraft delusions. No witch was ever hung there. . . . They treated the Indians with justice and good faith. They held no foot of land not fairly obtained by honest purchase. Their tolerance was an example to Roger Williams himself. And when at last in 1692, Plymouth was blended with Massachusetts, the days of bigotry and intolerance and superstition as a controlling force in Massachusetts were over." *(M.D. IV, 13).*

In the words of the Rev. Frederick B. Allen, "We are all Separatists now. There is not one of us here who is not thankful that throughout the length and breadth of the land there is no established church. It is largely because Protestants and Roman Catholics and Jews are all on precisely the same political level, in the sight of the law, that so kindly and charitable a spirit prevails between those of different faiths." *(M.D. IV, 8).*

The administration of the law by the Pilgrims was remarkably mild for the standards of their day. *(M.D. IV, 3).* The Pilgrims introduced much of our criminal code. When they lived, England had 149 capital crimes. The Pilgrims adopted only five which were practically the same as our laws today. They extended trial by jury so as to apply to all people. The Pilgrims established the public recording of deeds and mortgages and introduced our method of conveying land. They established the probating of wills and recording of births, marriages and deaths by towns. These were made applicable to all the people, a practice which had not previously existed. They introduced our system of administering estates. Instead of the oldest son inheriting all of his father's estate, the Pilgrims provided that the estate was to be divided equally among all children. This was a recognition of the rights of women. The Pilgrims introduced almost all of our system of equity. They introduced our system of free public education. Much of what they introduced was taken from the Dutch because no such institutions existed in England at that time *(NO. 66)*.

The Pilgrims were the only colonists who established a system whereby the people actually governed themselves. To avoid officialdom, they never elected any of their officers for a term of more than one year. They introduced local self-government as originally established in the township system. DeTocqueville said, "This system seems to have come directly from the hand of God." The first Declaration of Independence in America was formulated and ratified at a meeting of the General Court of New Plymouth, November 15, 1636. After reading their Compact and their Letters Patent of 1629, it was enacted: "We think good that it be established for an act: That . . . no imposition, law or ordinance be made or imposed upon or by ourselves or others at present, or to come, but such as shall be made or imposed by consent" of the voters.

In the Massachusetts Bay Colony at one period, not one man in four was a church member. There, as was the case in the New Haven Colony, only church members were allowed to vote. No such restriction was ever adopted in Plymouth. *(H XI 21)*.

"American self-government was not the sudden birth of the Declaration of Independence. For a century and a half the idea and political habits from which its strength was drawn had been gradually developed. According to Charles Borgeaud in his 'Rise of Democracy,' it 'really sprang from the organization which the Pilgrim Fathers gave to the first Colony, an organization which determined the shape and character of the State Constitutions which followed." *(BR 16)*.

THANKSGIVING DAY

Thanksgiving is a day which will be forever associated with the Pilgrims because they introduced it to America. It really was adopted from the Dutch who in turn had adopted it from the early Christians who in turn had taken it from the Bible in which the early thanksgivings of the Jewish people are described. The Dutch during their Eighty Years War with Spain used it to show their thanks to the Creator for His aid in the repelling of the invaders. The hymn, "The Prayer of Thanksgiving," was of Dutch origin and was first sung in the sixteenth century.

The first real day of Thanksgiving by the Pilgrims was when they were driven to take refuge on Clark's Island before the landing at Plymouth on Monday, December 21, 1620. The event is described by Bradford as follows: "for the next day was a faire sunshining day, and they found themsellvs to be on an iland secure from the Indeans, wher they might drie their stufe, fixe their peeces, and rest themselves, and gave God thanks for his mercies in their manifould deliverances. And this being the last day of the weeke, they prepared ther to keepe the Sabbath." *(B 104)*.

It was in 1623 that no rain fell between the third week in May and the middle of July. All of their plantings began to dry and wither because of the lack of water, and it seemed that all crops would be lost and famine would be their lot. The Indians appealed to their God for rain but in vain. Eventually the Pilgrims decided to call on their God by a day of humiliation and prayer *(M 64-65)*. Bradford describes what took place as follows: "Upon which they sett a parte a solemne day of humiliation, to seek the Lord by humble and fervente prayer, in this great distrese. And he was pleased to give them a gracious and speedy answer, both to thier owne and the Indeans admiration, that lived amongest them. For all the morning, and the greatest part of the day, it was clear weather and very hotte, and not a cloud or any signe of raine to be seen, yet toward evening it begane to overcast, and shortly after to raine, with shuch sweete and gentle showers, as gave them cause of rejoyceing and blessing God. It came, without either wind, or thunder, or any violence, and by degreese in that

11

abundance, as that the earth was thorowly wete and soked therwith. Which did so apparently revive and quicken the decayed corne and other fruits, as was wonderful to see, and the Indeans astonished to behold; and afterwards the Lord sent them shuch seasonable showers, with enterchange of faire warme weather, as, through his blessing, caused a fruitfull and liberall harvest, to ther no small comforte and rejoycing. For which mercie (in time conveniente) they also sett aparte a day of thanksgiveing." *(B 152-153).* In 1637, an ordinance was passed "that it be in the power of the governor and assistants to command solemn days of humiliation, and also for thanksgiving, as occasion shall be offered." *(Note M 13).* When the other New England colonies were formed, they eventually followed the example of Plymouth and fixed a certain day for Thanksgiving by formal proclamation.

Thanksgiving became a national day of observance when the Continental Congress on November 7, 1777, by formal proclamation, recommended that Thursday, December 18, 1777, be recognized as such. This action was probably motivated by the delegates from the New England colonies. When the British General Burgoyne was defeated at the Battle of Saratoga, Samuel Adams offered a resolution that a committee of three be appointed to prepare a recommendation to the several states to select a day for Thanksgiving "for the signal success lately obtained over the enemy of these United States." The resolution was adopted, and the three persons to serve on the committee were Samuel Adams, Richard Henry Lee and Col. Daniel Roberdeau. They were the drafters of a formal Proclamation which was subsequently adopted. This practice was continued annually by the Continental Congress until and including the year 1783. No day was thereafter set aside until on October 3, 1789, President George Washington, at the request of Congress, issued his first National Thanksgiving proclamation recommending and appointing Thursday, November 26, 1789, as the day. This was the last Thursday of the month.

Thereafter other dates were sometimes selected as follows: President George Washington issued on his own initiative a proclamation dated January 1, 1795, selecting Thursday, February 19, 1795, as the day; President John Adams in a Proclamation dated March 23, 1798, selected May 5, 1798; again in 1799, he selected Thursday, April 25, 1799; President Thomas Jefferson issued no proclamation; President James Madison by proclamation dated November 16, 1814, selected Thursday, January 12, 1815; again by proclamation dated March 4, 1815, he selected Thursday, April 13, 1815; and thereafter the practice was discontinued for forty-seven years.

On his own initiative, President Abraham Lincoln issued a formal proclamation dated April 10, 1862, selecting Sunday, April 13, 1862, as a day of National Thanksgiving. President James Buchanan, also President Lincoln, issued Proclamations for days of humiliation, fasting and prayer but these were not the same as Thanksgiving. In 1863 and 1864, President Lincoln followed the example of Washington and selected the last Thursday in November. In 1865, President Andrew Johnson selected Thursday, December 7, 1865, and in 1869, President Ulysses S. Grant selected Thursday, November 18, 1869. In 1870, President Grant changed back to the last Thursday in November, which was followed by all succeeding presidents, except for the times that President Franklin D. Roosevelt tried to move the day forward a week, causing two days frequently to be celebrated, the first, sometimes facetiously called "Franksgiving," on the earlier new official date, and an unofficial "Thanksgiving" on the last Thursday of November. Even President Roosevelt could not withstand the demand of the people that the day selected by Washington and followed by Lincoln should be selected again. So he reverted to the fourth Thursday in November, and so it has remained to the present time by act of Congress as a National day of Thanksgiving for everyone in the United States.

The Plymouth Settlement

The third exploring party of the "Mayflower" landed on December 21, 1620 (N.S.), at Plymouth, and the Pilgrims later began their settlement there in the wilderness. Their suffering was terrible. In the words of Governor Bradford, "But that which was most sadd & lamentable was, that in 2, or 3, moneths time halfe of their company dyed, espetialy in Jan. & February, being ye depth of winter, and wanting houses & other comforts; being infected with the scurvie & other diseases, which this long vioage & their inacomodate condition had brought upon them; so as ther dyed some times 2. or 3. of a day, in ye foresaid time; that of 100. & odd persons, scarce 50. remained. And of these in the time of most distress, ther was but 6. or 7. sound persons, who, to their great comendations be it spoken, spared no pains, night nor day, but with abundance of toyle and hazard of their owne health, fetched them woode, made them fires, drest them meat, made their beads, washed their lothsome cloaths, cloathd and uncloathed them; in a word, did all the homly & necessarie offices for them which dainty & quesie stomacks cannot endure to hear named; and all this willingly & cherfully, without any grudging in ye least, shewing herein their true love unto their freinds and bretheren." *(B 10)*. They were very often on the point of starving. It is related that they placed sick men with muskets on rests and with their backs leaning against trees to be a guard against possible attacks by the Indians when they had no well men who could be spared to stand guard *(PP 121)*. Their dead were buried in Cole's Hill, and later,

NOTE: Thanksgiving Day is appointed in each State by action of the Governor, and in the District of Columbia by statute fixing the fourth Thursday in November.

corn was planted over their graves that the Indians might not know how many were gone; yet their courage continued. In April, 1621, Christopher Jones, the Captain of the "Mayflower," which had remained in Plymouth harbor since December, offered to take back to England any who might wish to return, but such was their resolution and devotion to their ideal that not one of them went back.

Plymouth was the first successful settlement in any part of what later became the thirteen colonies. It is true that the Hudson River was discovered in 1609, and a trading post was built on the Island of Manhattan by the Dutch in 1613, but until 1624 the Dutch visited New Netherland only as traders. That year thirty families of Walloons settled on western Long Island. It was not until 1626 that all of the island of Manhattan was purchased from the Indians. Virginia was settled in 1607, but it was for many years a disastrous experiment. The success of the settlement at Plymouth encouraged the backers of the Virginia colonists to continue with their support *(Y 122)*. Governor Hutchinson said that it was the success of the Plymouth settlement that caused the Puritans to settle at Boston and other points in New England in and after 1630.

The question may be asked as to why the settlement at Plymouth succeeded in spite of what seems insurmountable obstacles. The answer may be found in the Pilgrim character. The earliest settlers of Virginia were largely adventurers who were unaccustomed to hard work and who sought their fortunes in the New World usually without their wives. The earliest Dutch settlers in Manhattan were traders. The Pilgrims, both men and women, were made of the material that could learn to work hard and could withstand all forms of persecution and death that they might worship God according to their consciences. In the New World they found religious freedom, and here they planted the permanent seeds of the New Nation.

When the Pilgrims came to the New World, they were

not the first white persons who had been to Plymouth. A map of the country had been made by Samuel de Champlain in 1605. The Pilgrims actually had in their possession a map made by Captain John Smith in 1614 on which the place of their future location is called "Plimouth" (B 94). There had been many other voyagers to those parts. On May 15, 1602, Bartholomew Gosnold discovered and named Cape Cod, because his party took much fish there. (B 95) (Y 101) (SV 31-50). The Cape kept this name in spite of the fact that John Smith in 1614 renamed it Cape James. In 1603, Martin Pring visited New England, then known as Northern Virginia (SV 51-63). In 1605, Captain George Waymouth came to New England (SV 98-151) as did Captain George Popham and Raleigh Gilbert in 1607 (SV 152-175). In 1609, Captain Henry Hudson visited Cape Cod (SV 176-192), and Captain Samuel Argall did the same in 1610 (SV 193-209). The latter is mentioned in a letter dated May 8, 1619, from Robert Cushman to the Leyden group in which Argall brings bad news concerning the Virginia settlement (B 59-60).

When Captain John Smith was off New England (SV 210-247), one of his captains, Thomas Hunt, took twenty of the Patuxet (Plymouth) Indians and also seven of the Nauset (Eastham) Indians as prisoners and sold them as slaves in Malaga, in the West Indies (M 41). The local friars caused them to be released, and one of them, named Squanto, made his way to England where he became a servant of Mr. John Slanie, a London merchant. When Thomas Dermer visited Plymouth in 1619 (SV 248-258), he brought Squanto back to his former home only for the latter to find that the Paauxet tribe had been swept away by disease (B 111, note). It was Squanto who, with Samoset, became a lasting friend of the Pilgrims. The hostility of the Indians was also largely aroused by a sea captain, alleged to be English, who a few years before the arrival of the Pilgrims had enticed a large group of peaceful

16

Indians on his ship only to murder them. When Captain
Dermer was on shore, he visited Plymouth as well as
Middleborough and Eastham because he left a description
of the soil in those places *(B 113)*. Of the many visitors to
these shores, Waymouth, Popham, Hudson, Argall, Smith
and Dermer left accounts of their voyages which were
published *(SV 98-258)* and which, with the exception of
Dermer's, might have been read by the Pilgrims before they
began their voyage. Bradford read Dermer's account after
the Pilgrims had settled in Plymouth *(B 111)*. Captain
Smith renamed Northern Virginia, New England. As already stated, he also named Plymouth *(B 112) (MD XXV
67)*. It is said that the Pilgrims were influenced to retain
the name because Plymouth, England, was the last town
they left in their native land and a place where many of
the people had shown much kindness *(M42)*. Smith may
have been influenced to give the name Plymouth to the
section because it was within the grant of the Plymouth
Company which in 1620 was reorganized as the Council
at Plymouth for New England. Plymouth is not on the
Cape. When the writer was a boy in Plymouth, he was
impressed that two statements especially annoyed the residents there. One was to say that the Pilgrims were Puritans; the other was to say that Plymouth is on the Cape.

The "Mayflower"

It has been said that the model of the "Mayflower" in
Pilgrim Hall, Plymouth, is the best model of the "May-
flower" in existence. It was made by R. C. Anderson of
Basset Holt, Southampton, England, who has been Vice-
President of the Society of Nautical Research, *(frontispiece
LH)*. There are two conflicting records concerning the ton-
nage of the "Mayflower." The "Mayflower" was a ship of
about 180 tons burden, according to Governor Bradford
(LH 16). Mr. Anderson, accepting Bradford's statement, cal-
culated length of keel, 64 feet; greatest beam, 26 feet inside

the planking; depth from beam to top of keel, 11 feet; and length from stem-post to stern-post, 90 feet. These dimensions give a ship of 183 tons burden or 244 gross tonnage, of the regular merchantman design *(LH 21)*.

In record 152 in the London Public Record Office may be found a note made by the Virginia Company showing ships sent to Virginia in 1620. Of six ships mentioned the third is the "May-Flower of 140 tuns in August 1620 with 100 persons" *(HS II 155)*. This means the "Mayflower" was even smaller than Bradford's figure.

The first plan was that the "Mayflower" would have ninety passengers. The ship brought more than this number because twelve more persons were added from those on the "Speedwell" when the latter vessel gave up the voyage *(DY 7)*. Oceanus Hopkins and Peregrine White were born on the voyage. The "Mayflower," small as she was, was a fine representative vessel, according to English possessions, for in 1587 there were not more than five merchant vessels exceeding 200 tons *(HXI 24)*. There were many other vessels at the time with the same name *(B Note 78) (LH 53)*. It was another "Mayflower" which came to Salem in 1629.

The Pilgrims landed from the "Mayflower" *(M 14)* first in Provincetown *(M.D. III 231)* where they obtained wood and water and refreshed themselves *(Y118, 123)*. After certain explorations they brought the "Mayflower" to Plymouth where they landed and settled. The rock was the place of their first permanent landing.

THE CREW

A vessel the size of the "Mayflower" would have had a crew of from twenty to twenty-five seamen in addition to the captain, mates, surgeon, petty officers and persons with special qualifications. The entire crew must have numbered between thirty-six and forty-one men *(DY 7)*.

PLYMOUTH ROCK TODAY

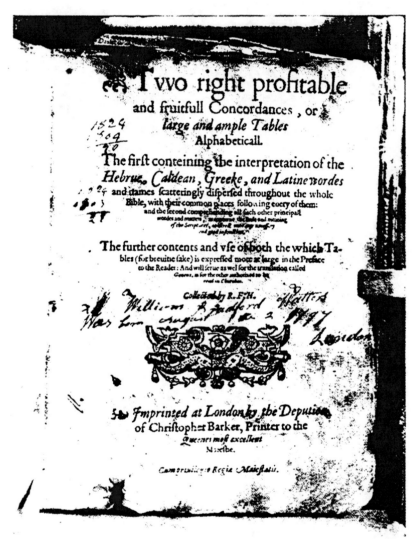

A PAGE FROM THE BIBLE OF WILLIAM BRADFORD

There has been some unnecessary confusion as to certain of the officers of the "Mayflower." The name of the captain was Christopher Jones, *(B, Note 87), (MJ, 669-680), (NE, XL, 62),* not Thomas Jones *(LH 18, 48-49).* It is stated that the kindness of Captain Jones was appreciated *(Y 138)* though Morton suspects him of duplicity *(M 21-22).* The first mate and pilot was John Clark *(B Note 75)* and not Thomas Clark, who came on the "Anne" in 1623. The second mate and pilot was Robert Coppin *(B 103)* and not Robert Coffin. Other mates were Andrew Williamson and John Parker *(K 19).* The surgeon was Dr. Giles Heale, who was of great help to the Pilgrims while the "Mayflower" remained at Plymouth. He was a witness to the will of William Mullins *(MD 1, 230-232) (NE 42, 62) (MA 38).* In the State Library at Richmond, Virginia, is a book, namely, a second edition of Henry Ainsworth's "Annotations upon the Book of Psalmes," published in 1617. On the front page appears the following: "This Booke was given unto me Giles Heale Cherugion by Isaacke Allerton Tailor in Virginia the X of February in the Yeare of our Lord 1620." This date in February 1621, according to our present method of keeping time, was just before Mrs. Allerton's death. At that time Virginia was considered as covering a vast territory which included New England *(B 65) (MD 34, 1-7).* The cooper of the ship was John Alden. The names of the remainder of the crew are unknown.

The question has been asked whether Captain Jones had been bribed to land the Pilgrims where he did. There is no direct evidence that he was. There is plenty of circumstantial evidence that something was wrong. Bradford never made the charge, but Morton on page 23 of his "Memorial" makes the allegation, and the facts seem to support his claim. The Pilgrims, according to Bradford, desired to find some place about "Hudson's" River for their habitation *(B 94).* The Dutch had been ready to accept them as Dutch settlers, but not as an English colony in what was later

New Jersey, a territory claimed by the English and by the Dutch. Captain Jones was experienced, and he had a copy of Captain John Smith's map of the coast. He must have known exactly what he was doing when he landed the Pilgrims on lands of the Plymouth Company, where their charter did not apply, instead of on the lands of the Virginia Company, to which their charter did apply. Once they arrived, they were too exhausted to move further. Morton's statement may be accepted as amply sustained by provable facts.

THE DATE OF THE LANDING

The Pilgrim method of fixing the day of the month differed from ours today. Prior to 1752, the civil year began on March 25, which was called the first month. April was the second month. The new style was introduced and has been continued since 1752. To render Old Style (O.S.) into New Style (N.S.), the first month must be accounted the third, and ten days be added to all dates between 1582 and 1700, and eleven days to dates between 1700 and 1752. For the single year, 1600, eleven days should be added.

The day of the landing by the third exploring party in the shallop at Plymouth was on the 11th day of December "O.S." This corresponds to the 21st day of December "N.S." as just explained *(M.D. I, 17-23)*.

PLYMOUTH ROCK

Thacher's "History of Plymouth" contains a good account of Plymouth Rock "The identical granite rock, upon which the sea-wearied Pilgrims from the 'Mayflower' first impressed their footsteps, has never been a subject of doubtful designation. The fact of its identity has been transmitted from father to son" *(T 29)*. James Thacher, who wrote the foregoing, was a famous Plymouth historian and was born in 1754. William S. Russell in his "Memorials" says, "The visitor frequently inquires, 'Is this the veritable rock which first received the Pilgrims?' Happily, we are able to answer his question with perfect confidence" *(R 18)*.

In considering the question of whether the Pilgrims actually landed on Plymouth Rock, we may well take up the likelihood of it. The Plymouth shore is sandy and flat, and it is difficult to land without stepping into the water, even from the flat-bottomed boats in use today. The difficulty would have been greatly increased by the fact that the boats in use at the time of the landing were round bottomed. Before locating the Rock, the Pilgrims complained that the shore was so shallow that the men were obliged to wade in water over their knees in going to and from their shallop, by which many had taken colds and coughs *(MR 5) (Y 120)*. The wading was called the cause of many of their deaths *(MR 68)*. It is reasonable to suppose that, to avoid stepping into the icy water, they would look along the shore for a rock that they might use, as a means to land without getting wet. The only rock in that vicinity was Plymouth Rock, which is not a native, but a fine-grained granite boulder, brought down and deposited by the ice-sheet, which once covered the greater part of eastern North America. This rock is near highwater mark, and owing to the many flats in the harbor, the exploring party would doubtless have come across from the island, where it had spent Sunday, when the tide was at its highest. The Rock was at the place where the Pilgrims landed according to the records. So much for the probability of the story.

Its authenticity rests on general and undisputed tradition and on certain well-defined statements transmitted from generation to generation *(Notes M 34-36)*. It was accentuated by the following event. Thomas Faunce, the last presiding elder of the First Church, was born in 1647 *(D 367)*. In 1741, when he was ninety-four years old, it was proposed to construct a wharf over the Rock, and he, supposing that it was to be buried away forever, was very anxious to see it

21

once more. He was brought down to the shore in a chair and there related how his father (who had come in the "Ann" in 1623) had told him that there was where the Pilgrims had first landed. He was old enough, too, to have heard the story from the Pilgrims themselves. He was nine years old when Standish died, ten years old when Bradford died, sixteen years old when Cooke died, twenty-six years old when Howland died and a man of thirty-eight when Samson died. He must have known twenty-three of the Pilgrims, and his mother was the sister of Nathaniel Morton, the colony historian. He thus had ample opportunity to verify his father's story. Ephraim Spooner, deacon of the First Church, told many times in his later life of being down at the Rock and hearing Faunce's story. The same information was communicated by Mrs. Joanna (Howland) White, a great granddaughter of John Howland and widow of Gideon White. She knew Elder Faunce well. She died 23 September 1810, age 95 years (R 19).

Edward Winslow, Jr., great-great-grandson of Governor Edward Winslow, was one of the founders of the Old Colony Club, which was founded in 1769 and which held, in the following year, what was probably the first official celebration of the Landing. On this occasion Winslow delivered the oration which described the landing on the Rock (T 184-185). Winslow was a contemporary of Deacon Spooner and must also have been associated in his daily life and in the club with many others who had been present when Elder Faunce formally identified the rock. We may assume, therefore, that Winslow was entirely familiar with the story. The first designation of the Rock on record is contained in a document in the second volume of Plymouth Town Records, page 181, dated in 1715, which refers to the "great rock" in a description of boundaries (R 29-30).

In July, 1774, Charles Blaskowitz, a Deputy Surveyor for the King for North America, presented Winslow with a pen and ink map of Plymouth Harbor. Upon this map, which is still preserved in Pilgrim Hall, Winslow himself made two notes. Near Clark's Island is written, "On this island the pious settlers of this Ancient Town first landed. . . . ."

The site of Plymouth Rock is marked "1" and near it is written "No. 1. The place where the settlers above mentioned first landed upon the main . . . upon a large rock . . . ."

These notes made by Winslow, and the information thus transmitted, may be regarded as the declaration of Elder Faunce and others, whose information was received from the Pilgrims themselves.

Mrs. Jane Palmer was born November 10, 1706, and lived to the age of 101 years. It was written that she, living but a short distance from the Rock, recollected frequently seeing it when quite young before the building of any wharf. Its form was described by her as being somewhat oval and regular and favorable for the uses which uniform tradition has always assigned it *(R 30)*. The Rock was not buried as Elder Faunce feared it might be. It was raised from its bed so that its top showed above the roadway of the wharf *(D 367)*.

Thacher gives the following story of its removal in 1774:

"The inhabitants of the town, animated by the glorious spirit of liberty which pervaded the Province and mindful of the precious relic of our forefathers, resolved to consecrate the rock on which they landed to the shrine of liberty. Col. Theophilus Cotton and a large number of inhabitants assembled, with about 20 yoke of oxen, for the purpose of its removal. The rock was elevated from its bed by means of large screws; and in attempting to mount it on the carriage, it split asunder, without any violence. As no one had observed a flaw, the circumstance occasioned some surprise. - - - The question was now to be decided whether both parts should be removed, and being decided in the negative, the bottom part was dropped again into its original bed, where it still remains, (1835) a few inches above the surface of the earth, at the head of the wharf." *(T 198-199)*. The upper portion was conveyed to Town Square in front of the church. The lower part remained upon the shore, and it was over this that the canopy was erected in 1859. The upper part remained in Town Square until July 4, 1834, when it was placed in front of Pilgrim Hall *(R 21)*. The following year an iron fence was placed around it for its protection and as a memorial to the Pilgrims. In 1880, the upper part was returned to the shore and was placed on the street level over where the lower part lay *(DH 174)*. Apparently the date "1620" was cut upon it at that time. There is pictorial evidence that the date appeared upon the Rock long before that, but it seems to have been painted upon it. In 1920, the wharves along the shore were removed, the Rock was lowered to its original level, and the present portico erected. The upper and lower parts of the Rock have been reunited and cemented together.

WHO LANDED FIRST

This question has been frequently asked, and it has never been satisfactorily answered. Confusion is increased because the landing might refer to several occasions. The first landing was at Provincetown on November 21, 1620. On the day of arrival, after the signing of the Compact, fifteen or sixteen men, well armed, were set ashore *(MR 8)*. Their names are unknown. On November 23rd, the women were permitted to go on shore to do their washing *(MR 12)*. On November 25th, the first exploratory expedition landed composed of sixteen men under Captain Myles Standish to whom were added William Bradford, Stephen Hopkins and Edward Tilley for counsel and advice *(MR 13-14)* *(B 98)*. The shallop having been repaired, a second expedition embarked in it on December 7th composed of twenty-four men and ten sailors *(MR 27)*. Their names are unknown.

After the return of the second expedition, a third left

24

the ship on December 16th. The names of its Pilgrim members have been preserved *(MR 43)*. They were Myles Standish, John Carver, William Bradford, Edward Winslow, John Tilley, Edward Tilley, John Howland, Richard Warren, Stephen Hopkins, Edward Doty, John Allerton, Thomas English, Mate John Clark, Pilot Robert Coppin, also the master gunner and three sailors, whose names are unknown *(M 31) (B 9, 100) (T 23)*. This group eventually landed at Plymouth on December 21st, and this is the occasion which is celebrated.

The "Mayflower," having been brought from Provincetown Harbor, anchored in Plymouth Harbor on December 26th, and the passengers remained on board on Sunday, December 27th. On December 28th a party landed *(MR 61-62)*, and on the 29th another party landed *(MR 63-64)*. On December 30th, about thirty persons landed, and it was determined to settle there *(MR 64)*. Thereafter as many as possible landed *(MR 66)*.

The claim that their ancestor was the first to land has been made by the descendants of both John Alden and Mary Chilton *(T 30)*, neither of whom was present at the landing of December 21st. Either could have been the first to land at Provincetown, namely John Alden among the men on November 21st and Mary Chilton among the women on November 23rd. There are no records to deny them this honor. Who landed first on December 21st is absolutely unknown except that he must have been one of the members of the third expedition who have been previously listed. Mary Chilton might have been the first woman to land on the rock when the women were permitted to land there. There are no records to dispute her claim while the authorities supporting her claim, based on tradition, have been collected and printed *(LI 6)*. There are no other claims except for these two.

It seems that the best answer to make to the question is that tradition claims that John Alden was the first man and

Mary Chilton, the first woman, who landed; that John Alden's landing was probably at Provincetown; that Mary Chilton's landing might have been either at Provincetown or Plymouth.

The Name "Pilgrims"

Why and when were the Separatists called "Pilgrims?" An early mention of "Pilgrims" is in the Epistle of Paul the Apostle to the Hebrews *(Chapter XI, Verses, 13-16)*. "These all died in faith, not having received the promises, but having seen them afar off, and were persuaded of them, and embraced them, and confessed that they were strangers and pilgrims on the earth. For they that say such things declare plainly that they seek a country. And truly if they had been mindful of that country from whence they came out, they might have had opportunity to have returned. But now they desire a better country, that is, an heavenly: wherefore God is not ashamed to be called their God: for he hath prepared for them a city."

It was obviously this reference which caused Bradford to write, "but they knew they were pilgrimes, and looked not much on those things, but lift up their eyes to the heavens, their dearest countries and quieted their spirits" *(B 79)*. This expression was copied by Nathaniel Morton in the Church Records *(CR 43)*. It was copied by Cotton Mather and perhaps other writers. The term "Pilgrims" first began to be used to distinguish the "Mayflower" passengers about 1798 and thereafter came more and more into use in common speech. The "Massachusetts Mercury" for December 27, 1799, contains an account of the Feast of the Sons of the Pilgrims on Forefather's Day, 1799 *(M.D. I, 113-114)*. This subject has been described at length by Albert Matthews *(MT 293-391)*.

The Pilgrim Society was organized in Plymouth in 1819 and was incorporated in 1820. Daniel Webster constantly mentioned the Pilgrims in his famous speech delivered at the anniversary celebrated in December of the latter year. "America," which refers to "land of the Pilgrim's pride," was written in 1832. Thacher's "History of Plymouth," First Edition, published in 1832, shows that the term had been in common use for some time.

THE PASSENGERS

There is no mystery concerning the last names of the passengers on the "Mayflower" except as to one maid-servant. Bradford has left a complete list *(Appendix A)*. I remember someone telling me with great pride concerning the name of "Green" and that there were five Greens who came over on the "Mayflower." I told her that I regretted to tell her that no Green came over on the "Mayflower." At certain meetings of the Society of Mayflower Descendants, the Compact is read aloud, after which the names of the signers are read and each descendant is asked to rise when his or her ancestor's name is called. A large number will arise when John Alden's name is read, but hardly anyone arises when the name of William Mullens, his father-in-law, is read. Of course, everyone descended from Alden is also descended from Mullens. When the name of Edward Tilley is called, before that of John Tilley, a large group will arise even though he left no descendants. Of course, he is confused with his brother, from whom all John Howland descendants are descended. The following is a list of all male heads of families coming on the "Mayflower" from whom descent has been proved. I recommend it being used at Mayflower gatherings, not only because persons who left no descendants have been eliminated, but also because the names of certain persons are included who were children and hence never signed the Mayflower Compact:

John Alden	William Brewster
Isaac Allerton	Peter Brown
John Billington	James Chilton
William Bradford	Francis Cooke

Edward Doty	Degory Priest
Francis Eaton	Thomas Rogers
Edward Fuller	Henry Samson
Samuel Fuller	George Soule
Stephen Hopkins	Myles Standish
John Howland	John Tilley
Richard More	Richard Warren
William Mullins	William White

Edward Winslow   *(M.D. I, 126-127)*.

Governor Bradford wrote his account of the "Mayflower" passengers and their "decreasings and increasings" during the four weeks between March 6, 1651, and April 3, 1651 (new style), *(M.D. I, 161-163)*. Banks claims that Bradford in making his list of passengers forgot two names, namely, Giles Heale and one Master Leaver. I think that Bradford knew better than the late Banks who came over as passengers in the "Mayflower." Heale, as ship's surgeon, was a member of the crew and not a passenger. Master Leaver, described as a member of a rescue party on January 12, 1620/21 in Mourt's "Relation" *(MR 74)*, may have been an officer of the "Mayflower" because the name does not re-appear after the vessel returned to England, and some of the other mates are also referred to therein as Master when they similarly accompanied the Pilgrims on their expeditions. Certain authorities, however, believe that the name was a misspelling of Carver. There is no just ground for questioning the correctness of Governor Bradford's list.

MISREPRESENTATIONS ABOUT THE PILGRIMS

Detractors of the Pilgrims have seized upon several events which have been used as a basis for misrepresentations. A few years ago an opera was produced by the Metropolitan Opera Company in New York City which depicted the renegade Thomas Morton of Merry Mount as a royalist hero and the Pilgrims as Puritan persecutors of royalists and Shakers, the latter a sect organized in England in 1758 and

28

which came to America in 1774, long after all the Pilgrims were dead. Needless to say, the whole plot was imaginary and not similar in any important particular to what really occurred.

In 1628, at Mount Wallaston (near present Quincy), renamed "Merry Mount," one Thomas Morton gathered about him a dissolute group of men servants, who had left their masters, and who took part in drunken carousals with Indian women, causing scandal among their neighbors. The Pilgrims could have closed their eyes to this situation, but when Thomas Morton engaged in the business of supplying guns and ammunition to the Indians, the situation was serious *(B 237-243)*. Standish with men from Plymouth arrested Morton, and he was returned a prisoner to England. The merits of the matter may be appreciated when one learns that practically every settlement contributed toward the expense of sending him back to England *(M.D. VI, 207-211)*. His supplying guns and ammunition to the Indians made him a menace, and all of the settlements united to get rid of him in their own defense. At the time all this occurred, there were no royalists as such in America, and the Shaker or even the Quaker movement had not been born.

Another matter which detractors have misrepresented is what happened between the Pilgrims and the Massachusetts Indians in 1623. News had come of the massacre of 347 of the colonists in Virginia by Indians *(B 139) (HL 165)* on March 22, 1622. When Winslow had cured Massasoit from an illness, that chieftain divulged that the Massachusetts Indians were arranging to exterminate Weston's colony and the Plymouth colony thereafter. He advised that the Pilgrims strike the first blow. The matter was considered at length by the Plymouth colonists with the result that Standish and eight men with their friend Hobomak went against the Massachusetts Indians in order to secure their leader, the arch conspirator Wattamat. Pecksuot and other Indians joined the latter in threatening the Pilgrim group with knives and with insulting speeches and gestures. The situation was serious, and Standish did what seemed to him the best that could be done. Standish arranged so as to get Pecksuot, Wattamat, the latter's brother, and another Indian into a room in which were about an equal number of his own men. Locking the door, Standish killed Pecksuot in a fair fight with the Indian's own knife while Standish's companions killed two of the others. The brother was taken prisoner and later hanged. With his army of nine, Standish again attacked in another place, killing one more Indian. Later, meeting a file of Indians, he put them to rout, challenging the sachem to a single combat, which was refused *(Y 310-311; 337-339) (T 55-56)*. The facts of the conspiracy were fully substantiated by later confessions. Standish, by killing the few conspirators, saved the lives of all the whites from certain destruction. This was the last real trouble that the Plymouth people had with the Indians until King Philip's War, over fifty years later. This is a remarkable record *(MD XXVI 129)*.

Governor Josiah Winslow, when referring to lands obtained from the Indians, said, "we do not claim an acre of land, not fairly purchased of the Indians: or for which we had not their free consent." President John Adams and James Otis confirmed this statement in 1770 *(NT 437)*.

Mention has been made that the Pilgrims brought beer on the Mayflower. This they did according to English custom, but its use seems to have been discontinued when they found they could get pure water. There is no record of their ever having a brewery or of sending to England for any more beer.

Another matter that has been misrepresented has been the relations of the Plymouth people with the Quakers. The Pilgrims had never persecuted anyone because of his religion. Equally they desired to be left undisturbed in the practice of their religion. The Quaker movement began about 1656, and its adherents soon got into trouble with the authorities. Some of them went about urging the people not to patronize the existing churches, alleging the ministers taught lies. Sometimes some of them went to the Plymouth churches in order to break up the meetings by disputing with the clergymen during their services. They refused to pay tithes or to take an oath of allegiance. They refused to serve in the army though the Indian danger made compulsory military service necessary. Some of them reviled the magistrates when brought before them. Most of what they did that was objectionable would be punished today under the head of disorderly conduct and contempt of court. Their treatment in Plymouth was due to their conduct and not to their religion.

It has been said that the Pilgrims objected to taking oaths. The Pilgrims had not only no objection to taking oaths, but even made them obligatory. In a memorandum to Sir John Wolstenholme, a member of the Virginia company, the Reverend John Robinson and Elder William Brewster wrote that their group would take the oath of supremacy if the oath of allegiance did not suffice. *(B 56)*. In Plymouth the Pilgrims required an oath of allegiance, another from every resident and an additional oath from every office holder.

"For eighteen years all laws were enacted in a general assembly of all the colonists. The Governor, chosen annually, was but president of a council, in which he had a double vote. It consisted first of one, then of five and finally of seven counselors, called assistants.

"The constitution of the Church was equally democratic. For the first eight years there was no pastor, unless Robinson, still in Holland, might be considered in that light. Brewster, the ruling elder, and such private members as had the gift of prophecy, officiated as exhorters. On Sunday afternoons a question was propounded, to which all spoke who had anything to say" *(HL 175)*.

The First Parish Church

The First Parish Church in Plymouth is the Church of the Pilgrims, who arrived in Plymouth on the "Mayflower," December 21, 1620.

In the early history of the Plymouth Colony, the town and Parish were one. By the setting off of parts of the original territorial parish as separate precincts and parishes, it became the First Precinct, or Parish, in Plymouth. Since 1786, it has been a corporation by virtue of a statute of the General Court. *(From the Preamble to the By-Laws of the First Parish in Plymouth).*

The Church Covenants
Scrooby - 1606

"As ye Lord's free people, we joyne ourselves, by a covenant of the Lord, in ye fellowship of ye gospell, to walke in all his ways, made known, or to be made known unto us, according to our best endeavors, whatsoever it shall cost us, the Lord assisting us." *(Adapted from Bradford)* *(B 31).*

Holland - 1620

"We promise and covenant with God and one with another to receive whatsoever light or truth shall be made*to us from his written word." *(Adapted from Winslow).*

Plymouth - 1676

'In the name of our Lord Jesus Christ & in obedience to his Holy will and divine ordinances:

"We being by the most wise & good Providence of God brought together in this place & desirous to unite ourselves into one congregation or church under the Lord Jesus Christ, our Head, that it may be in such sort as becometh

32

---

*See page 196.

all those whom He hath redeemed & sanctified to himself, Wee do hereby solemly & religiously (as in his most holy presence) avouch the Lord Jehovah the only true God to be our God & the God of ours & doe promise & binde ourselves to walke in all our wayes, according to the Rule or the Gospel & in all sincere conformity to His holy ordinances & in mutual love to, & watchfulness over one another, depending wholy & only upon the Lord our God to enable us by his grace hereunto." *(The Records of the First Church) (RC I 148).*

Until 1744 town meetings handled-matters of the Church. The word "Unitarian" does not appear in the Church records earlier than June, 1828 (CRI Int. XLVI).

A question has arisen whether the First Church at Plymouth should take 1620 as its date of origin, or whether it was the original congregation which was organized in Scrooby in 1606, fled to Holland and later came to Plymouth. The historian Arthur Lord in "Plymouth and the Pilgrims," pages 103-104, gives the following reason for selecting the 1620 date:

"One other problem waited solution and that was to determine who of the Leyden Church were to go and who to remain.

"It was further determined that those who went should become an 'absolute' or independent church, and those who remained should continue the existing organization."

The date, therefore, of the organization of the first church in Plymouth has been fixed as in the year 1620, and not in the year 1606, when the first members of the congregation assembled at Scrooby. "In accordance with the congregational way, it was agreed, if any returned to Leyden or if any from Leyden thereafter went to America, no letters of dismissal or testimonial would be necessary to enable them to unite either with the church at Leyden or with the church in America."

This means that the Plymouth Church is an offshoot of

the original church, but the question may well be asked as to why the Plymouth Church, as more and more members of the Leyden congregation joined it, did not become the main and only church when the Leyden Church ceased to have any existence.

EDUCATION OF CHILDREN

The first allusion to education was on January 25, 1623, when some of their adversaries residing in London said of them, "Children not catechized nor taught to read." This was answered as follows: "Neither is true; for diverse take pain with their owne as they can; indeede, we have no commone schoole for want of a fitt person, or hitherto means to maintaine one, though we desire now to begine." *(B 170)*. The record states that all the charges were answered and duly sent to London, greatly to the shame and confusion of all those who had been instrumental in so groundless a slander. *(R 176)*. The same matter of education appears in the Church Records *(CR 52-53)*.

The Colony originally was principally indebted for the means of education to the learned and venerable clergy. On February 11, 1635, the Old Colony Records state that "Benjamin Eaton, with his mother's consent, is put to Bridget Fuller (the widow of Dr. Samuel Fuller) being to keep him at school two years, and employ him after in such service as she saw good, and he may be fit for." In June, 1662, the court recommended to the consideration of the several towns some preparations for schools; and in 1663, it made the following enactment: "It is proposed by the Court unto the several township in this jurisdiction, as a thing they ought to take into their serious consideration, that some course may be taken that in every town there may be a schoolmaster set up to train up children in reading and writing." *(R 176-178)*. In 1668, John Morton offered "to teach children and youth of the town to read and write and cast accounts on reasonable considerations."

In 1670, a grant was made for a free school. In August, 1671, John Morton appeared at a town meeting and renewed his proposal to erect and keep a town school which was accepted. In 1672, the profits of the Cape Cod fishery and other ventures were paid to Thomas Hinckley, steward and treasurer of the school toward its maintenance. It is thought that this was perhaps the first free school ordained by law in New England. (T 302). The Massachusetts Bay Colony law of 1647, providing for schools, provided for a reasonable tax on the scholars at the discretion of the towns.

In 1672, a Mr. Corlet was the instructor, and he gave a higher standard of instruction including Latin and Greek. Notice was again taken of the free school by the General Court in 1675. Thereafter the town records show the continued maintenance of the free school where all children could be educated without expense to them.

It may be seen that from the earliest times the inhabitants of Plymouth appreciated the necessity of education and that they strove to overcome obstacles so as to have proper schools.

PILGRIM SPELLING

Some persons have tried to show that nearly all of the early settlers, including the Pilgrims, were uneducated because they did not spell correctly.

Such statements are historically untrue.

Attempts were made in the late sixteenth century to standardize spelling, and a good deal of regularity was achieved, especially by printers, so that by the middle of the seventeenth century our present spelling practices had become generally established for published books. There was, however, if one can judge from the letters and manuscripts of many people of the time, no strong sense of "right" and "wrong" in spelling, and inconsistencies occur frequently in documents written by educated people.

It is sometimes difficult to determine, however, whether a special spelling is phonetic or is one of several spellings for a word which has survived from the late Middle English period, when the various dialect regions had their own spellings. Even after the London dialect became the standard in the early fifteenth century, regional spellings for some words appeared in manuscripts and later in the first printed books.

If one counts the actual number of words which might be phonetic spellings in Governor Bradford's "History," the proportion of such spellings to variations established by custom (sometimes several for one word) is not large. In other words, Bradford and others of his time were not themselves consciously reproducing sounds of words as they wrote them, but using a spelling they had often seen. These spellings often go back to a time in the fourteenth century when spelling actually was fairly phonetic. Many of the early American colonists were well-read people, and no one in his own time would have criticized their spellings. It was not until after the middle of the eighteenth century that English spelling was taught in schools. Johnson's dictionary was the first one to stress right spelling as such.

A good account of spelling in the sixteenth and seventeenth centuries appears in Albert Baugh's "History of the English Language."

Pilgrim Houses

There have been many mis-statements concerning the houses of the Pilgrims. The original houses at Plymouth were constructed of boards not logs. They never lived in log cabins. The ordinary Pilgrim houses had thatched roofs, vertically boarded plank walls and stone floors. The Pilgrims built their houses as they knew them in England, (GR). They brought the tools for building with them, including saws and nails. Their accounts show that as soon as possible they had dug pits for the sawing of boards for home building purposes and for export *(DY 15)*. Bradford records that the "Fortune" returned to England in 1621 "being laden with good clapboard as full as she could stowe" *(B 123)*.

In the earliest days of Plymouth, the settlement consisted of the first (now Leyden) street with twelve houses, a common storehouse, and the governor's house. These structures were surrounded by a palisade, with a fort dominating the scene from the nearby hill. The fort was connected with the village by a palisade *(PX)*.

"Pilgrims' Progress"

Many visitors to Plymouth have seen the "Pilgrims' Progress" enacted by local descendants of the Pilgrims. At the sound of a drum on certain afternoons during each summer, a group of men, women and children, dressed as their ancestors had dressed, with the men carrying guns, gather at the foot of Leyden Street and go from thence, led by those taking the parts of Governor, Elder and Captain, to the top of Burial Hill where a service is held, conducted by the Elder. After the service, they retrace their steps to whence they came. It is an affecting sight, and people come from long distances to witness it. The basis of it is a record left by Isaac De Rasiere, a wise observer from Holland in 1627, part of which is as follows:

"Upon the hill they had a large square house, with a flat roof, made of thick sawn planks, stayed with oak beams, upon the top of which they have six cannons, which shoot iron balls of four and five pounds, and command the surrounding country. The lower part they use for their church, where they preach on Sundays and the usual holidays. They assemble by beat of drum, each with his musket or firelock, in front of the captain's door; they have their cloaks on, and place themselves in order, three abreast, and are led by a sergeant without beat of drum. Behind comes the Goevrnor, in a long robe; beside him on the right hand

37

comes the preacher with his cloak on, and on the left hand
the Captain with his side-arms and cloak on, and with a
small cane in his hand; and so they march in good order,
and each sets his arms down near him. Thus they enter
their place of worship, constantly on guard night and day"
(M. D. IV, 103 (R 131-150).

While the writer was Governor of the New York Society
of Mayflower Descendants, he had the costumes used in
Plymouth copied so that a series of scenes from Pilgrim
history were depicted by members of the New York Society.
The following year, certain of the younger members enacted
the "Pilgrims' Progress" at a Mayflower Society dinner held
in one of the local hotels, and it was most impressive. There
seems no good reason why the "Pilgrims' Progress" in cos-
tume should not be enacted by descendants at their gatherings in any part of the United States.

COMMUNISM

Certain persons have intimated that the Pilgrims practiced Communism. There has been an attempt to create the
impression that they were believers in some form of it. The
very opposite is the truth.

When the Pilgrims first landed, they were compelled to
hold land and goods in common because of their agreement
with the Merchant Adventurers. In the spring of 1623,
Governor Bradford and the Pilgrim community abandoned
this system, and his condemnation of communism is about
as strong as could be expressed in words.

The people in 1622 were too weak from want of food to
tend the crops as they should. "So as it well appeared,"
writes Governor Bradford, "that famine must still insue
the next year allso, if not some way prevented. *(B 139).* So
they begane to thinke (in 1623) how they might raise as
much corne as they could, and obtaine a beter crope than
they had done, that they might not still thus languish in
miserie. At length after much debate of things, the Govn

(with the advise of the cheefest amongest them) gave way that they should set corne every man for his owne particuler, and in that regard trust to them selves;" "And so assigned to every family a parcel of land - - -

"This had very good success; for it made all hands very industrious, so as much more corne was planted than other waise would have bene by any means the Govn or any other could use, and saved him a great deall of trouble, and gave far better contents. The women now wente willingly into field and tooke their little-ons with them to set corne, which would aledg weaknes and inabilities; whom to have compelled would have bene thought great tiranie and oppression.

"The experience that was had in this commone course and condition, tried sudrie years, and that amongst godly and sober men, may well evince the vanitie of that conceite of Platos and other ancients, applauded by some of later times; — that the taking away of propertie, and bringing in communitie into comone wealth, would make them happy and florishing; as if they were wiser than God. For this communitie (so farr as it was) was found to breed much confusion and discontent and retard much imployment that would have been to their benefits and comforte. For the yong-men that were most able and fitte for lobour and service did repine that they should spend their time and streingth to worke for other mens wives and children, without any recompense. The strong, or man of part, had no more in division of victails and cloaths, than he that was weake and not able to doe a quarter the other could; this was thought injuestice. - - -

"And for men's wives to be commanded to doe service for other men, as dressing their meate, washing their cloaths, etc., they deemd it a kind of slaverie, neither could many husbands well brooke it" *(B 146-147).* Bradford later continues concerning the fall.

"By this time harvest was come, and instead of famine,

now God gave them plentie, and the face of things was changed, to the rejoysing of the harts of many, for which they blessed God. And the effect of their particular planting was well seene, for all had, one way and other, pretty well to bring the year aboute, and some of the abler sorte and more industrious had to spare, and sell to others, so as any generall wante or famine hath not been amoungest them since to this day." *(B 157)*.

The experiences of the Pilgrims as set forth by Bradford show that Communism brought them want and poverty while individual ownership of property brought them plenty and success. The Pilgrims never tried this disastrous experiment again.

THE NAME OF THE "MAYFLOWER"

It is remarkable that neither Bradford's "History" nor Mourt's "Relation" mention the name of the "Mayflower." The fact that the vessel on which they came was named the "Mayflower" is known from a reference in the Plymouth Colony Record of Deeds in the handwriting of Bradford made in 1623 in which is stated the vessel's name. The earliest American mention in print is in Nathaniel Morton's "New England's Memorial" published in 1669. The latter writer must have been personally acquainted with nearly one-half of the "Mayflower" passengers *(M. D. V, 114)*, and two of them were alive when he wrote his account. Thus he was in a position to obtain the facts from those who knew them. The earliest English record is when the vessel is named in record 152 in the London Public Record Office made by the Virginia Company *(HS II 155)*.

GRAVESTONES

It has been stated in print that the oldest gravestone on Burial Hill goes back only to 1703. This statement is based on hearsay which has no factual basis. *(R 69)*. The oldest gravestone on Burial Hill is that of Edward Gray, Gent., who died on June 30, 1681 *(D.R. 95) (K 3)*. The next oldest gravestone is that of William Crowe, which shows that he died in January, 1683. *(K 4)*. The gravestone of Mrs. Hannah Clark shows that she died February 20, 1687 *(K 4)*. The gravestone of "Mr." Thomas Clark shows that he died March 24, 1697. The gravestone of Nathaniel Thomas, son of Nathaniel Thomas, "Esq.," shows that he died on April 15, 1697 *(K 7)*. Thomas Cushman died in 1691, but in his case the gravestone was not erected until twenty-four years after his death. *(M.D. IV, 37)*. There exists no historical account of the time when this hill first became the place of sepulture. It has, however, been inferred from traditions which have come down, that it was so used not long after 1622, when the fort was constructed and served for public worship as well as defense. Why gravestones were not sooner placed there can now only be a subject of conjecture *(R 65)*. It may be significant that it was not until all danger from Indian attack had passed that gravestones were erected. It may be of interest to consider the causes which impelled the Pilgrims not to erect gravestones at an earlier date. When the Pilgrims were losing many persons by death during the first terrible winter, they buried their dead as best they could and eventually planted grain over their graves on Cole's Hill in order that the Indians might not know how many were gone. After they had made their peace with Massasoit and had built their homes in various localities, there might have been a fear that prowling Indians might interfere with the graves if they were marked. There probably remained the desire to conceal from the Indians the number of their dead. While graves near the fort would probably have not been molested, nevertheless, gravestones near the fort would have furnished convenient protection for an enemy attacking the fort. Once the custom based on good reasons had been originated for not marking their graves, the practice continued until, as previously shown, danger from Indian attack had passed away.

41

Principal Events

In order to have a quick reference to the principal events after the "Mayflower" sailed, the following table is inserted. It should be remembered that the Pilgrims used "old style" in writing their dates so that it has been necessary to change them to "new style" to correspond with our present calendar.

1620

August 15 — Sailed from Southampton, England.

September 16 — Sailed from Plymouth, England.

November 19 — First sighted Cape Cod.

November 21 — Signed the Compact.
Anchored in Cape Cod Harbor and went ashore.

November 23 — Took the shallop ashore for repairs.

November 25 — First exploring party set out by land.

November 26 — Discovered Truro Springs, Pamet River, Cornhill.

December 7 — Second exploring party set out with the shallop.

December 10 — Found the wigwams, graves, etc.

December 16 — Third exploring party set out with the shallop.

December 18 — First encounter with the Indians.
Reached Clark's Island at night.

December 20 — Third exploring party spent the Sabbath on Clark's Island.

December 21 — Third exploring party landed, using Plymouth Rock, and explored the coast.

December 25 — The "Mayflower" set sail from Cape Cod for Plymouth, but was driven back by a change in the wind.

December 26 — The "Mayflower" arrived at Plymouth Harbor.

December 27 — First Sabbath passed by the whole company in Plymouth Harbor.

December 28 — A party landed and explored the land.

December 29 — One party explored by land and another in the shallop. Discovered Jones River.

December 30 — Decided to settle near what is now Burial Hill along Town Brook.

1621

March 26 — Samoset came among them alone.

March 28 — Samoset came again with five others.

April 1 — Samoset and Squanto came to announce the coming of Massasoit with whom a treaty was made.

"Beginning of April" — The "Mayflower" sailed in order to return to England *(M.D. I, 86-89).*

ANNIVERSARY CELEBRATIONS

The hundredth anniversary of the landing of the Pilgrims came and went, so far as we can learn, quite unnoticed and unmarked. For many years after the landing of the Pilgrims there was no organization which preserved their memories or their ideals. The Old Colony Club was formed in Plymouth on January 16, 1769, with the following unique constitution.

"We whose names are underwritten having maturely weighed and seriously considered the many advantages and inconveniences that arise from intermixing with the company in the taverns in this town, and apprehending that a well regulated club will have a tendency to prevent the same, and to increase, not only the pleasure and happiness of the respective members, but also, will conduce to their edification and instruction, do hereby incorporate ourselves into a society, by the name of the Old Colony Club. For the better regulation of which we do consent and agree to observe all such rules and laws, as shall from time to time

43

be made by the club. Dated at our Hall, in Plymouth, the day and year above written.

Isaac Lothrop	John Thomas
Pelham Winslow	Edward Winslow, Jr.
Thomas Lothrop	John Watson"
Elikanah Cushman	

The historian Thacher states: "It was in this club that the custom of solemnizing the anniversary of the arrival of our forefathers first originated and this was the principal object of its formation." *(T 180-181)*. The club held weekly meetings.

On December 22, 1769, was held the first celebration of the landing of the Pilgrims. The members went from old Colony Hall to the inn of Consider Howland, brother-in-law of the senior Edward Winslow, where the following repast was served. It is especially interesting as showing what constituted a Pilgrim meal in the opinion of these men.

"1. a large baked Indian whortleberry pudding;
2. a dish of sauquetach (succotash, corn and beans boiled together);
3. a dish of clams;
4. a dish of oysters and a dish of codfish;
5. a haunch of venison, roasted by the first Jack brought to the Colony;
6. a dish of sea fowl;
7. a dish of frost fish and eels;
8. an apple pie;
9. a course of cranberry tarts, and cheese made in the Old Colony." *(T 181-182)*.

Edward Winslow, Jr., delivered the oration, and there was also a poem by Alexander Scammell.

That evening at a meeting the following additional members were elected and joined the Club *(T 182)*:

Col. George Watson	Capt. Thomas Davis
Col. James Warren	Dr. Nathaniel Lothrop

James Hovey, Esq.	Mr. John Russell
Thomas Mayhew, Esq.	Mr. Edward Clarke
William Watson, Esq.	Mr. Alexander Scammell
Capt. Gideon White	Mr. Peleg Wadsworth
Capt. Elkanah Watson	Mr. Thomas Southworth Howland

Thereafter the Old Colony Club celebrated the landing of the Pilgrims on December 24, 1770, and on December 23, 1771. On December 22, 1772, Chandler Robbins conducted the celebration for the Old Colony Club. Meanwhile the Continental Congress had appointed Committees of Correspondence and Communication throughout the Colonies, and the one formed in Plymouth determined to take a leading part in the celebration to be held in December, 1773. Members of the club were on the Committee while other members remained loyal to their king. The Club held a dinner and meeting on December 22, 1773, but it was its last. The celebration was conducted by the Rev. Charles Turner for the Old Colony Club, by the town and by the first parish. The Old Colony Club was thereafter dissolved because of differences between its members caused by the coming Revolution.

The Committee of Correspondence and Communication included names of men who had been leaders in the Old Colony Club. The Committee was appointed on November 24, 1772, at a legal meeting of the town. The members were:

James Warren	Elkanah Watson
John Torrey	William Watson
Stephen Sampson	Thomas Lothrop
Samuel Cole	Nathaniel Torrey
Ephraim Cobb	Thomas Mayhew
Dr. William Thomas	Isaac Lothrop
Thomas Jackson	

It was in 1774 that the Rock was moved as elsewhere described herein. During the ensuing few years, political conditions left no time for extensive or elaborate celebrations. The celebration held on December 22, 1774, was just a sermon by The Rev. Gad Hitchcock of Pembroke. He was followed in 1775 by the Rev. Samuel Baldwin of Hanover; 1776, by the Rev. Sylvanus Conant of Middleborough; 1777, the Rev. Samuel West of Dartmouth; 1778, the Rev. Timothy Hilliard of Barnstable; 1779, the Rev. William Shaw of Marshfield; and in 1780, the Rev. Jonathan Moor of Rochester *(T-339)*.

From this time the public observances of the landing were suspended until 1794 when the Rev. Chandler Robbins of Plymouth celebrated the occasion. In 1795, 1796 and 1797, there were private celebrations. In 1798, Dr. Zaccheus Bartlett of Plymouth delivered the oration. That year there was a celebration in Boston. In 1799, the day came so near that appointed for the ordination of the Rev. James Kendall that it was not celebrated in Plymouth by a public discourse. Thereafter orations at Plymouth were delivered as follows: 1800, Hon. John Davis; 1801, Rev. John Allyn; 1802, Hon. John Quincy Adams, eventually to be President of the United States; 1803, Rev. John Thornton Kirkland, President of Harvard; 1804, Rev. James Kendall; 1805, Hon. Alden Bradford, Secretary of the Commonwealth; 1806, Rev. Abiel Holmes; 1807, Rev. James Freeman; 1808, Rev. Thaddeus M. Harris; 1809, Rev. Abiel Abbott; 1811, Rev. John Eliot, one of the founders of the Massachusetts Historical Society; 1815, Rev. James Flint; 1817, Rev. Horace Holley; 1818, Hon. Wendell Davis; and in 1819, Hon. Francis C. Gray.

In 1805, the New England Society was founded in New York City which celebrated the anniversary of the landing. There was also formed a New England Society in Charleston, South Carolina.

In 1819, a group of public spirited persons organized the Pilgrim Society which was incorporated on Feb. 24, 1820. Its purpose was to commemorate the Pilgrims and to perpetuate their character and virtues. One of the first acts of the Society was to erect Pilgrim Hall which preserves on

46

public view many objects closely associated with the Pilgrims. The Hon. Joshua Thomas, a descendant of John Alden, was the first president. Several honorary members were elected, among them being the Rev. James Kendall, Hon. Isaac Parker, Lt. Governor William Phillips, Governor John Brooks and former President John Adams.

Before the first celebration conducted by the Society, an attempt was made to get Joseph Story as the orator. He was unable to act. So the brilliant young Boston lawyer, formerly a Congressman from New Hampshire, Daniel Webster, was selected, and the result helped to make the remarkable reputation which he thereafter enjoyed. His career in the United States Senate and as Secretary of State was to come later. The celebration was opened by a prayer offered by the Rev. Dr. John T. Kirkland, President of Harvard University. Then Webster delivered his remarkable oration concerning the Pilgrims. It will live forever. The newly formed "Standish Guards," now a part of the National Guard, aided in the occasion. The guests then sat down to a dinner held in the new Plymouth Court House, where five kernels of parched corn were placed on each plate to remind them of the sufferings of the Pilgrims. Judge Joshua Thomas, President of the Pilgrim Society, could not be present because of an illness which proved to be his last. The presiding officer was the venerable John Watson, who was the only surviving member of the Old Colony Club. There were distinguished speakers, and the occasion was most successful. The celebration ended with a ball in the evening (T 232-238). There has been preserved a souvenir of the dinner.

Many persons have probably seen blue china plates which show an imaginary landing of the "Mayflower" group. John Alden is shown stepping first upon the rock while two Indians are standing on the shore, one of them with arms outstretched as if in welcome. These may be assumed to be Samoset and Squanto. Upon the rock may be read the names of Carver, Bradford, Winslow, Brewster and Standish. The border of the design comprises a sketch of the national eagle together with scrolls encircling the later historic dates, "America Independent, July 4, 1776," and "Washington Born 1732, Died 1799."

I had received a rumor that some such plates had been used at the dinner held in connection with the celebration in Plymouth in 1810. I investigated and found the answer in "The Blue-China Book" by Ada Walker Camehl. Dinner sets with this design were made in 1820 in the pottery of Enoch Wood, in Staffordshire, England, and are considered some of his best work. They were sent to the United States in large quantities as souvenirs at the many bi-centennial celebrations that were being held that year. The banquet, held in Plymouth, was served upon one of the souvenir dinner sets. It is believed that the diners were permitted to keep their plates. While the scene of the landing is historically inaccurate, nevertheless, the plates are most interesting by recalling the very wonderful celebration held in Plymouth in 1820. Moore in "The Old China Book," page 21, states that these pieces are always in demand.

The next celebration by the Pilgrim Society was in 1824 when Edward Everett delivered the oration. Josiah Quincy had been asked first to deliver it, but he asked to be excused. In 1829, the Society asked Harrison Gray Otis to deliver the oration. He had declined previously on another occasion, and he again expressed his inability to do it. Apparently no oration was delivered that year. In 1831, the Rev. John Brazer of Salem delivered a sermon at the first Parish Church. For many years a memorial sermon was considered an appropriate method of celebration.

In 1845, the Pilgrim Society celebrated the 225th Anniversary with a procession in addition to the ceremonies (HG) (PW) See also (DA) and (DC) for subsequent years. The same thing was done in 1870 when the 250th anniversary was celebrated. In 1895, the same was done for the

275th anniversary. On December 21, 1920, Senator Henry Cabot Lodge delivered his magnificent oration *(WZ)*. In 1921, Plymouth town, its citizens, the Pilgrim Society, everyone united in one of the most outstanding celebrations that could be given. The year 1921 was selected because it was necessary to have the celebration during the summer time, and it was thought that it would be more appropriate and easier to have it in 1921 than in 1920.

The whole waterfront of the town in the vicinity of the Rock was changed. Instead of a dirty wharf section of the town, the harbor and wharves in the vicinity of the Rock were filled in and covered with dirt so as to make parks on either side of the Rock. So far as the celebration itself was concerned, the outstanding event was the pageant. For many months almost one thousand persons from Plymouth and the adjacent towns rehearsed, and then in August they performed the pageant for a period of approximately three weeks to enormous crowds. President Warren G. Harding and many dignitaries of the nation attended. A parade was held which was reviewed by the President. The writer marched in it with the Veteran Corps of Artillery from New York. Outstanding speakers graced the occasion. Not the least contribution to the success of the gathering was the commemorative poem concerning the Pilgrims written by LeBaron R. Briggs. The performers in the pageant were trained by Professor George Pierce Baker of Harvard, and no one could have done better The whole occasion was most successful and brought the greatest credit to Plymouth and to the memory of the Pilgrims. In other years the Pilgrim Society has continued its practice of having some distinguished speaker at the annual celebration.

The Pilgrim Record Society

The first organization, formed outside of Plymouth to commemorate especially the Pilgrims, which I have been able to locate, was the Pilgrim Record Society, which today is almost unknown. This Society seems to have been formed on December 30, 1875. Prior to that date, David P. Holton, M.D., was the Secretary of the American Philological Society. His office was at 19 Great Jones Street, opposite Lafayette Place, New York City. As an offshoot of the American Philological Society, Dr. Holton seems to have organized the Pilgrim Record Society. An extract from its bylaws is as follows:

"2. The material, gradually accumulated by several family committees shall form the basis of a common genealogy of all the Pilgrim descendants in which all the less extended data shall be included, while those families which present complete and carefully compiled histories will be aided by the influence of the General Society in making known throughout the country their approaching publications, stamped with its authoritative approval."

The Society issued a Bulletin which bore on its cover the following:

"In the interest of a Method in genealogical studies, and for the publication of family pedigrees and histories."

The Society held its meetings at 19 Great Jones Street, on the second Tuescday evening of each month. Dr. Holton was secretary of the Society.

The first anniversary of the Society was held in Room 18, Cooper Institute, on Saturday evening, December 30, 1876. Miles Standish was elected president, and Hon. Frank Fuller, 137 Eighth Street, was treasurer. The annual dues were $5.00, Life Membership $50, and subscription to the Bulletin was $1.00 for twenty numbers. Dr. Holton was Editor and Publisher of the Bulletin.

In the New York Public Library are copies of the first seven numbers of the Bulletin issue in 1876, and a Union Bulletin of the American Philological Society and the Pilgrim Record Society (1 issue).

The Bulletin contains very extensive records of a Diary

ALDEN HOUSE, DUXBURY

HOWLAND HOUSE, PLYMOUTH

CABINET BELONGING TO WHITE

CHAIR BELONGING TO BREWSTER

of Mary Chilton and articles about other "Mayflower" Pilgrims such as the Winslow Family.

It seems likely that the American Philological Society records would contain information as to what happened to the Pilgrim Record Society. It was apparently a special hobby of Dr. Holton, as Miles Standish in his inaugural address before the Society on December 30, 1876, stated that he had accepted the office only because of the urging of Dr. Holton and that his resignation was already on file. The American Philological Society seemed to have had some activity in Philadelphia and held a convention in August, 1876. The purpose of that Society had solely to do with the English language and its use. In 1878, the Pilgrim Record Society was located at 61 East 59th Street, New York City. I have no record of its end.

The Society of Mayflower Descendants

The Society of Mayflower Descendants had its origin in the State of New York where an organization was formed on December 22, 1894, by a group of descendants who saw other societies in existence which celebrated the memories of other persons and events prominent in American history, but none of which recalled the Pilgrims or that for which they stood. The New York organization was successful from its beginning. Societies were formed in Connecticut on March 7, 1896, and in Massachusetts on March 28, 1896, and in Pennsylvania on July 1, 1896. Representatives of these state societies met and arranged to form a general society, which was organized at Plymouth on January 12, 1897. It was incorporated under the laws of the Commonwealth of Massachusetts on February 19, 1923.

Other state societies were quickly organized thereafter. The General Board of Assistants chartered the Society in the State of Illinois on June 1, 1897, and those of the District of Columbia and Ohio on March 22, 1898. The New Jersey Society received its charter on August 15, 1900. The

Wisconsin Society received its charter on January 26; the Rhode Island Society and the Michigan Society on February 8; and the Maine Society on September 6, 1901. The Colorado Society followed with a charter granted on April 21, 1906. The enthusiasm moved to the Pacific coast where the California Society received a charter on October 17, 1907, and the State of Washington on March 28, 1912. The Kansas Society received a charter on November 21, 1914, and the Indiana Society one on March 21, 1916. The Nebraska Society followed with a charter granted on December 16, 1922.

The society invaded the South when the North Carolina Society was chartered on September 2, 1924. The Vermont Society received its charter on August 19, 1927. The next year saw the chartering of three state societies: namely, Iowa on March 27, Missouri on April 14, and Oregon on December 28. The Georgia Society received its charter on October 31, 1929, and the New Hampshire Society on August 5, 1930. The Minnesota Society received its charter on December 11, 1931, and the Texas Society on December 24th of the same year. The Florida Society received its charter on July 31, 1937. The Maryland Society received its charter on March 4th, and the South Carolina Society on July 1, 1938. The Kentucky Society received its charter on October 27, 1943, and the Louisiana Society received its charter on July 14, 1945. The Idaho Society received its charter on November 21, 1946, and the next year witnessed the Mississippi Society receiving its charter on January 29th, and the Oklahoma Society its charter on March 29, 1947. The North Dakota Society received its charter on October 26, 1947; the Tennessee Society, on August 28, 1948; the Utah Society, on November 5, 1948; the West Virginia, on November 6, 1948; and the Virginia Society, on January 10, 1950. It is hoped to form organizations in every state, and also in the Hawaiian Islands. The record is truly remarkable.

The objects for which the General Society of Mayflower Descendants has been formed are:

"Section 1. To perpetuate to a remote posterity the memory of our Pilgrim Fathers. To maintain and defend the principle of civil and religious liberty as set forth in the Compact of the Mayflower, 'For the glorie of God and the advancemente of the Christian Faith, and honor of our countrie.'

Section 2. To cherish and maintain the ideals and institutions of American freedom, and to oppose any theories or actions that threaten their continuity.

To transmit the spirit, the purity of purpose and steadfastness of will of the Pilgrim Fathers to those who shall come after us, an undiminished heritage of liberty and law.

Section 3. To promote the interests that are common to all the State Societies of Mayflower Descendants which can best be served by a federal body and to secure unified efforts to discover and publish with existing data known only to antiquarians, and to authenticate, preserve and mark historical spots made memorable by Pilgrim association."

The Society of Mayflower Descendants has been a success from the beginning. It has been a useful part of every community in which a branch is located. Copies of the Compact have been distributed by it among schools, churches, clubs and colleges. Hundreds of thousands of the copies have been sent to teachers so that over a million school children have been yearly told the great lesson of the Compact. Truly if the great lesson of love, toleration and respect for one's fellow man, as evidenced in the Compact, had guided the world, there would have been no more wars and the world's nations would have cooperated for the benefit of all. People have asked me, "What good do the patriotic societies such as the Society of Mayflower Descendants accomplish?" Not only are these organizations trying to maintain organized support for our government in the future by teaching the lessons learned from the past, but also in my experience, I have had three occasions when these societies were of the greatest value in times of crisis. In 1917, the New York National Guard was ordered to a southern camp, and there was no law that permitted a State guard to be formed in its place. That meant that valuable war facilities must go unprotected unless something was done. There was one old patriotic organization that had a charter that antedated the militia law and which permitted its members to bear arms. A group of men, of which I was one, at the request of the Adjutant General, used the charter to recruit a regiment of 1400 men from members of the patriotic societies in New York, and these men took over the guarding of the extensive water system of New York City, previously guarded by the National Guard. Eventually the law was amended and a State Guard was formed. The patriotic societies had proved themselves to be organized groups of loyal Americans who were ready in any emergency.

When the second World War came, I was told by Mayor Fiorello H. LaGuardia of New York City that I must furnish the names of several hundred outstandingly honest men to serve on draft boards and that I must send in the names within twenty-four hours. I went to the patriotic and veteran societies and next morning sent by messenger the names of about 300 men to the Mayor, many of whom served to the end of the war.

The third incident was when during the second World War, the Mayor asked me to form a force of 3000 men to help the police in guarding military objectives. My task was to find the men and to select all the officers. I went to the patriotic and veteran societies, and I organized the New York City Patrol Corps, which eventually comprised over 8,000 uniformed and well-drilled persons who took over the guarding of military objectives and who patrolled in dangerous areas. I might not have succeeded in what I did if I had not had organizations of real Americans like the Society of Mayflower Descendants upon which to call when the crisis came. The patriotic societies are definitely a benefit and a source of strength to the country generally. They can be called upon in any emergency.

The various State organizations maintain the interests of their members by holding meetings which are both interesting and instructive. Many Mayflower descendants moving to other localities have joined a local society in the new location and have thereby acquired a large number of outstanding friends. The Mayflower Society has succeeded in attracting to its membership many of the leaders and persons of importance in every State. One of the greatest pleasures that any one can have is to attend the triennial Congresses at Plymouth where the delegates from the State Societies act as the General Society. There, in Plymouth, in the home of their forbears, the descendants consider at these Congresses how their combined effort may redound to the benefit of these United States. The Mayflower Society is a live organization that has endeavored to be a credit to our country. I cannot close this phase of my account without mentioning the kindly good feeling that exists among the members. They realize, that coming from the small Plymouth group, the probabilities are that most of them are related in some degree.

MAYFLOWER SOCIETY HOUSE

At this point it will be interesting if I describe the very beautiful home which the General Society of Mayflower Descendants owns in the town of Plymouth.

North Street was laid out by the early settlers before the year 1633, and in the deeds was referred to as New Street, Queen Street, Howland Street and after 1823, as North Street. The name Howland was given to the street because of the large number of members of that family who owned land there. Indeed the land upon which the Edward Winslow House stands was one of the early Howland holdings. The first of the family was the Pilgrim John Howland. His son, Captain Joseph Howland, a prominent Plymouth resident, married Elizabeth, daughter of Captain Thomas Southworth, and is the first known owner of the land upon which the house stands. At his death, his son, Captain Thomas Howland, a large Plymouth land owner, inherited the Winslow House land. Thomas Howland married Joanna, daughter of James Cole, who kept a famous inn. Their son, Consider Howland, inherited his grandfather Cole's business, and his inn became a center of activity and town life. Consider inherited the Winslow House land from his father. In 1741, Edward Winslow married Hannah, daughter of Captain Thomas Howland and in 1754, he bought from his brother-in-law, Consider, the land upon which he, the next year, built his house.

Edward Winslow, who caused the house to be built, was the sixth child of Isaac and Sarah (Wensley) Winslow, who are hereinafter described. He was born in Marshfield on January 7, 1714, surrounded by all of the advantages obtainable by wealth and social position. He became "an accomplished scholar and a gentleman of fine taste." He was graduated from Harvard College with the degree of A.B. in 1736. All students at Harvard were graded at that time according to the social position of their families, a practice which continued to exist to and including the class of 1772. Edward Winslow was graded first in a class of twenty-seven students, which fact evidences his high social position. He was later awarded the degree of A.M. He soon settled in Plymouth where he became town clerk in March, 1740, and where he married Hannah, widow of Charles Dyer, and daughter of Captain Thomas Howland as previously mentioned. Edward Winslow only continued to be town clerk until January 1742 *(PTR)*.

56

It is said that when he built his house, the frame and some of the paneling were brought from England *(MX 3)*. Here he lived with his wife and three children, Edward, Penelope and Sally, as benefitted his high position in society. He was lavish in his entertainments and generous to the poor. There were other wealthy and socially prominent families in the town of Plymouth, such as the Warren, Howland, Thomas, LeBaron, Lothrop, Watson, Cushman, White, Davis, Russell, Cotton, Spooner, and Robbins families. These families made a pleasant society in Plymouth, which town was recognized as being one of the most cultured centers in the Colony. Other outstanding families, such as the Severs of Kingston, were in the neighboring towns. Edward Winslow held many offices in Plymouth, among them Clerk of the Courts, Register of Probate and Collector of the Port of Plymouth. His son, Edward, Jr., was graduated from Harvard in 1765, being ranked sixth in a class of fifty-four students. The student ranked socially first was Nathaniel Sparhawk, Jr., grandson of the great hero of the capture of Louisburg from the French, Lieutenant General Sir William Pepperell Bart. This son Edward was an intelligent and accomplished gentleman. It was he who became one of the founders of the Old Colony Club and who delivered the oration at the first celebration of the landing of the Pilgrims, which Thacher has included in his history. *(T 184-185)*. Everything seemed calm until there came the events leading to the American Revolution.

The members of the Winslow family were intensely loyal to their king. There were other Loyalists in Plymouth, but the Whigs overwhelmingly outnumbered them. The center of Loyalist agitation was in Edward Winslow's home town of Marshfield, where there had been formed an organization called the "Associated Loyalists of Marshfield" with an enrollment of 300 members, inspired and dominated by one Nathaniel Ray Thomas and Dr. Isaac Winslow, son of General John Winslow and nephew of Edward. The meetings of the group were held in the Winslow House in Marshfield. The influence of these men was far reaching.

Nathaniel Ray Thomas, descendant of William Thomas, one of the Merchant Adventurers who financed the "Mayflower," was graduated from Harvard in 1751 where he was ranked seventh in a class of thirty-five. He was the proprietor of the largest estate in Plymouth County and had inherited great wealth. He became a dominant factor in the control of the policies of the people of Marshfield which had some effect on Plymouth. Eventually the British made him a Mandamus Counsellor. Dr. Isaac Winslow, Harvard Class of 1762, was the beloved physician of Marshfield, and he had a large family connection by birth and marriage. Edward Winslow was a close friend of these men.

These Loyalists brought to Marshfield and stored a large quantity of tea until the "Boston Tea Party" in December, 1773, brought matters to a crisis. A few days later a group of Whigs went at midnight with ox carts and seized the tea. Later it was burned. Nathaniel Ray Thomas tried in vain to get the town to pay for it. In September, 1774, the citizens of Pembroke, Scituate and Hanover united with those of Marshfield and marched to arrest Nathaniel Ray Thomas, but he had fled. He did not return until after a company of the Queens Guards, under command of Captain Balfour, was sent down and quartered in Nathaniel Ray Thomas' houses at the urgent request of himself and other Loyalists who feared for their lives and property. These troops landed from the North River on December 20, 1774, and were a most imposing sight as they marched by the Training Green in fine array, their red coats and shining bayonets glittering in the sun, on their way to their quarters on the Thomas estate. The presence of these troops was greatly resented, and their arrogant demeanor and not always exemplary conduct roused the ire of the people. It was while dining with Edward Winslow in Plymouth that the following incident took place.

Captain Balfour and his officers soon made themselves acquainted with the friends of the royal cause in Plymouth. Their visits were not pleasing to the Tories, as the Whig party was known to be in a state of such ferment that a small spark might kindle a blaze and create a fatal collision. Captain Balfour and his officers were, however, invited to dine with Edward Winslow in company with a number of respectable gentlemen of their party in Plymouth. Captain Balfour desired to have the opinion of the company present on the expediency of marching his company of guards into Plymouth. In discussing the subject, one of the gentlemen, Mr. John Watson, was observed to be silent. Captain Balfour took him aside and said, "Mr. Watson, I observed that you gave no opinion respecting my proposal; I should be glad to have your opinion and advice on the subject."

Mr. Watson replied, "It is my opinion that it will not be prudent to bring your company here, for the people are in a state of great excitement and alarm."

"Will they fight?" asked Balfour.

"Yes," replied Watson, "like devils."

On further consideration, the plan was wisely abandoned from an appreciation of the consequences. (*T 205-206*).

Edward Winslow, Jr., living in the old house, was soon in trouble because of his Tory activities. Sabine's "Loyalists of the American Revolution" tells how in 1774, the Plymouth County Convention resolved: "That Edward Winslow, Jr., one of the two clerks of the Court of General Sessions of the Peace and Court of Common Pleas for this county, has, by refusing this body a copy of an Address made at the last term in this county to Thomas Hutchinson, Esq., betrayed the trust imposed in him, and by refusing his attendance when requested, treated the body of this county with insult and contempt, and by that means rendered himself unworthy to serve the country in the said office." In 1775, he joined the royal army in Boston and, entering the King's service, he became a colonel.

When the news of Lexington and Concord came, concerted action by the American militia was planned against the British troops in Marshfield. Before it could be done successfully, Captain Balfour and his troops retreated to Brant Rock where British-men-of-war were lying in readiness to rescue them. It is said that Captain Balfour's company was later practically annihilated at the battle of Bunker Hill as only five and their captain survived. Nathaniel Ray Thomas, who had returned with the troops, departed with them in April, 1775, never to return.

In a footnote on page 328, Volume 2, of the printed records of the Town of Plymouth, it appears that Edward Winslow was removed from his various town offices in 1775. He moved to Boston soon after the fighting began. There he signed a "Loyal Address," dated October 6, 1775, from gentlemen and principal inhabitants of Boston to Governor Gage on the latter's departure for England. Stark's "The Loyalists of Massachusetts" shows that Edward Winslow and Mrs. Hannah Winslow were among the refugees who went to Halifax with the army after the evacuation of Boston by the British on March 17, 1776. Sabine also so states. Edward Winslow did not stay long in Canada. The fighting moved southward; he returned to Plymouth with his wife and lived there quietly during the remainder of the war, with some small interruptions as hereinafter described.

At a meeting of the Town of Plymouth held on June 16, 1777, the Selectmen presented the following report:

"In Pursuance of a Late Act of the Generall Assembly of the State of Massachusetts Bay, We the Subscribers Selectmen of the Town of Plymouth (with the Advice and Concurrence of the Committee of Correspondence) do Present to the town the following list of Persons belonging to sd town whom we apprehend have been Endeavoring

Since the 19th of April 1775 to Counter Act the Struggles of this & the United States for the Preservation of their Liberties & previleges viz

John Watson	Gideon White
Edward Winslow	Ichabod Shaw
	Edward Davis

Plimouth June 16th 1777." *(PTR III 329).*

The Committee appointed by the town to collect evidence against the Tories reported on June 23, 1777, as follows:

"Against Edward Winslow, Esqr. Mr. Winslow acknowledged to the Committee of Correspondence that some time about the first of May last Mr. Bethell came from Rhode Island to this town and was at his house. Sd Bethell we look upon as an open Enimy to America. Mr. Joshua Thomas says that Mr. Winslow Pleaded in Excuse for not Informg of Said Bethell that he had Bonds from the bord of Commissioners to make up all his loss, occasioned by the Boston Port bill." *(PTR III 331).*

At the town meeting, those attending voted against having Edward Winslow tried. *(PTR III 333).* The Committee of Correspondence continued to watch him with the following result:

"To Thomas Mayhew, Esq., one of the Justices of the Peace in the County of Plymouth:—

"I, the Subscriber, clerk of the Committee of Correspondence, inspection and safety for the town of Plymouth, truly represent to you as a Justice of the Peace in the county aforesaid, that there is in the opinion of said committee, sufficient reason to suspect that the following persons, viz., Edward Winslow and George Watson, Esquires, Captain Gideon White, John Watson, Benjamin Churchill, Captain Thomas Davis, Captain Barnabas Hedge, Isaac LeBaron, Samuel Hunt, Ichabod Shaw, John Kempton, John Kempton, Jr., Zaccheus Kempton, Benjamin Ryder, William LeBaron, Enoch Randall, William Cuffee, Jerry Connel,

61

Richard Durfey, Lemuel Cobb, and James Doten, Jr., are inimical to the United States, and you are requested, upon this representation, to proceed immediately against the above named persons, agreeably to an Act of said State passed the present session of the General Court, entitled an act for prescribing and establishing an oath of fidelity and allegiance.

"By order of the Committee of Correspondence,
Andrew Croswell,
Clerk.

Plymouth, 11th February, 1778" *(D 188).*

Thomas Mayhew issued his warrant to the Sheriff of the County to notify the persons named to appear the next day to take the prescribed oath. These alleged Tories, having complied with the requirements of the law, were liberated and subsequently were considered among the town's most peaceable and useful citizens. *(T 210).* Edward Winslow continued to live in Plymouth in his house.

It is related that a harassed British officer rode his horse in the front door of the Winslow house and out the back. One version is that the horse tried to go upstairs. One British officer of a group from Marshfield aroused the resentment of a "mob" on Main Street. Umbrage was taken by some of the watchful sons of liberty, one of whom claimed that the officer had menaced, with a drawn sword, an individual in the street. The crowd present was ready to avenge the fancied insult. The officer was obliged to retreat and entered an apothecary shop kept by a Tory, Dr. Hicks, for safety. The crowd surrounded the shop and demanded the officer's sword. So insistent was the mob that the sword was taken by force from the officer and broken into several pieces. *(T 206).* Later the officer succeeded in running across back lots to take refuge in the Winslow house where he remained safe until he could leave Plymouth and return to Marshfield after dark.

On January 1, 1781, Edward Winslow was required by

law to contribute 1 pound 4 shillings and sixpence to procure a soldier for the Continental Army. *(PTR III 407)*. The surrender of Lord Cornwallis and his troops and the capture of Yorktown by the Americans on October 19, 1781, was decisive and showed that the British cause was hopeless. In December, 1781, Edward Winslow joined the British garrison in New York City with part of his family, the remainder joining him later. Sir Henry Clinton allowed him a pension of 200 pounds per annum with rations and fuel. On August 13, 1783, with wife, two daughters and three colored servants, he sailed for Halifax, reaching there on September 14, 1783. He died there in 1784.

Edward Winslow, Jr., had been proscribed and banished. He went to Lexington with Lord Percy on April 19, 1775, in the effort to rescue the British troops retreating from Concord. He was appointed by General Gage, Collector of the Port of Boston and Register of Probate of Suffolk County. He was one of the signers of a "Loyal Address to Governor Gage" on his departure for England dated October 14, 1775, "by those gentlemen who were driven from their habitations in the Country to the Town of Boston." Like his parents, he went to Halifax with the British Army when the latter evacuated Boston on March 17, 1776. In Halifax he was made by Sir William Howe, Secretary of the Board of General Officers, of which Lord Percy was President, for distribution of donations to the troops. After the British had captured New York, he went there and was appointed Muster Master General of the forces and remained in the United States in that capacity during the war except that in 1779 he was chosen by the refugees in Rhode Island to command them, which he did during two campaigns. After the war, Edward Winslow, Jr., was Military Secretary in Halifax until 1785 when he moved to New Brunswick and was a member of the first King's Council formed in that Colony, Surrogate General, Judge of Supreme Court and finally Administrator of the

Government. He died at Frederickton, in New Brunswick, in May, 1815. He had three children. His son, Edward, was drowned, and another son, Wentworth, survived him. He had a daughter Penelope. His descendants are still living in Canada. None of them has ever lived again in Plymouth.

When Edward Winslow, Senior, died, his funeral in Halifax was attended by all of the dignitaries of the city. On his tombstone in St. Paul's churchyard it is stated that "he in no one instant degenerated in the loyalty or virtue of (his) ancestors."

The house, which is popularly supposed to have been confiscated, was really taken on execution by creditors consisting of the town of Plymouth, also Thomas Davis, Dr. William Thomas, Oakes Angier and John Rowe who had supplied the money on which the Winslow family lived after Edward Winslow had lost his offices *(MY 6)*. When Edward Winslow definitely abandoned Plymouth, the creditors sold the house in 1782 to Thomas Jackson. *(DM 24-25)*. When Winslow learned of this, he was very angry, claiming that the whole of his property was taken and sold for less than half the value thereof. Other deeds were given in 1789, 1790 and 1791.

The main creditor seems to have been Dr. William Thomas, who had been as active for the colonists as his cousin Nathaniel Ray Thomas had been for the king. He was a descendant from the Merchant Adventurer, William Thomas, and his wife was a descendant of John Alden. He was a first cousin of the mother of Paul Revere. The old doctor had been surgeon during the French and Indian Wars. When the news of Lexington came and Colonel Theophilus Cotton's regiment marched from Plymouth, the doctor was surgeon; his son Joshua was adjutant; his son John was surgeon's mate. His other sons Nathaniel and Joseph entered the service, two of the sons becoming original members of the Society of the Cincinnati.

His lawyer son Joshua Thomas, Harvard 1772, had been

discharged from the army after serving in the 26th Continental Infantry during the siege of Boston and on the staff of General John Thomas in the attack on Canada. Joshua conducted the legal proceedings leading to the taking over of the house, which thereafter was never again inhabited by Tories. Thomas Jackson, purchaser of the house, had been born in 1757, and in 1788 married Sarah May, a descendant of Richard Warren. They had three children. Thomas Jackson owned the house until 1813 when it passed under an execution to his first cousin Charles Jackson, born in 1770 and who in 1794 married Lucy Cotton, not only a descendant of Richard Warren, but also of Josiah Winslow, brother of Pilgrim Edward. She was a niece of Colonel Theophilus Cotton, commander of the first Plymouth regiment to leave for the front in the Revolution. Mr. Jackson lived in the house until his death in 1818. Dr. James Thacher lived there for a time *(DM 276)*. Mr. and Mrs. Charles Jackson had several children who lived in the old house, of whom two became particularly distinguished. His daughter Lydia, sometimes called Lidian, was born in 1802. During the early part of the nineteenth century it was quite usual for famous men to come to Plymouth to lecture, during which visit they would stay with one of the local prominent families. In 1833, Ralph Waldo Emerson, having lost his first wife by death in February 1831, came to Plymouth to lecture in Pilgrim Hall on "Socrates." The visit was probably suggested by young Dr. LeBaron Russell of Plymouth who was an intimate friend of Emerson for the greater part of his life. He was the guest of LeBaron's father, Nathaniel Russell, whose daughter, Mary Howland Russell, was an intimate friend of Lydia Jackson. The historian Davis believes that this was the first time that Emerson saw his future wife.

Dr. LeBaron Russell has left an interesting account of one of the incidents of Emerson's life. He has given some particulars concerning the introduction of Thomas Carlyle's "Sartor Resartus" to American readers. This appeared in "Frasers," and Emerson lent the copies of the magazine to Lydia Jackson in the Winslow House and the work caused great excitement among the young persons in Plymouth who were interested in the literature of the day. Dr. Russell desired to own a copy and consulted a publisher concerning an American edition. He wrote to Emerson and asked if he would write a preface. This Emerson did, and James Monroe and Company issued the first American edition in 1836. Carlyle could find no English publisher who at first would assume the responsibility of publishing the book. *(EH 81-82)*. With Emerson's preface to the American publication, the first edition was entirely sold and a thousand copies besides, before it was published in book form in England *(E XXIV)*. Taine's "History of English Literature" describes "Sartor Resartus" as a clothes-philosophy which "contains, a propos of aprons and breeches, a metaphysics, a politics, a psychology. Man according to him, is a dressed animal. Society has clothes for its foundation. 'How, without clothes, could we possess the master-organ, soul's seat, and true pinial gland of the Body Social: I mean, a Purse.'" The quotation is from "Sartor Resartus," Book I, Chapter X; Pure Reason. It shows what interested the young Plymouth people of that day. The public appreciated to the utmost the preface written by Emerson, and his reputation continued to grow.

Emerson went to live with his mother in the "Old Manse" in Concord in October, 1834. This house had been built by his grandfather, the Rev. William Emerson, minister of the Concord Church, and his mother was living there with her venerable step-father the Rev. Ezra Ripley.

When Emerson became engaged to Lydia Jackson, he bought at a bargain the Coolidge house in Concord. He drove from Concord to Plymouth and, on August 22, 1835, was married to Lydia Jackson in the East front room of her Plymouth home with Dr. LeBaron Russell and his sister Mary Howland Russell acting as "best man" and "maid of honor." *(EH 83)*. After their marriage Mr. and Mrs. Emerson went to live in his Concord house where they resided for the remainder of their lives.

His wife Lydia "would have liked to have lived in Plymouth, but he preferred Concord, and had written to her that 'he was born a poet, though his singing was very husky and for the most part in prose,' and therefore must guard and study his rambling propensities. Concord, he intimated gave him sunsets, forests, snow storms, and river views, which were more to him than friends, but Plymouth! —'Plymouth is streets.'" *(E XXIII)*. It was thus that Emerson scornfully referred to our revered Leyden, Middle, North, Main and Court Streets in Plymouth. Perhaps a better reason for his choosing Concord was that his family had long been prominent there. Also he had obtained a position preaching at the neighboring East Lexington Church, where he continued to preach during the winters of 1835 and 1836 while giving his famous lectures on English literature when not engaged in the ministry. It was in Concord that a most remarkable group of intellectuals gathered under the leadership of the Emersons, which included at various times Margaret Fuller, Amos Bronson Alcott with his gifted daughter Louisa M. Alcott, Henry David Thoreau, Nathaniel Hawthorne and others.

Lydia's brother, Charles Thomas Jackson, was born on June 21, 1805, and was graduated from the Harvard Medical School in 1829. He studied for three years in Europe, returning in 1832. He received many honors and was responsible for developing the copper mines on Lake Superior. It is claimed that he was the first one to suggest correspondence by means of electricity perfected by Morse. He was a co-discoverer with Dr. William T. G. Morton of anasthesia *(MY 6-7)*. The brilliant Charles Thomas Jackson died in 1880. *(DM 273-274)*. In 1872, the Jackson heirs sold the house to the wife of the Reverend George Ware Briggs, who had been "colleague pastor" with the Reverend James Kendall in Plymouth from 1838 and remained there until 1852 *(D 104)*. Thereafter Mr. and Mrs. Briggs used it as a summer residence. Mrs. Briggs was a sister of Dr. LeBaron Russell and of Mary Howland Russell who introduced Ralph Waldo Emerson to his future wife. She died on November 1, 1881, and Mr. Briggs died in Plymouth on September 12, 1895, leaving two sons, George Russell Briggs and LeBaron Russell Briggs who lived in the old house. The former was the father of Miss Rose Thornton Briggs, the Plymouth antiquarian, who has done so much for Plymouth and who has maintained her interest in the house. The latter son is the late beloved Dean of Harvard College and President of Radcliffe College who lived in the house many summers during his latter years. Mrs. George W. Briggs was a descendant of William Bradford and of John Howland. She was descended from the latter through Consider Howland who sold the land upon which the house stands to his brother-in-law Edward Winslow.

In 1898, the house was purchased by Mr. Charles L. Willoughby, a wealthy resident of Chicago. He was inspired by its history to undertake the task of restoration. He employed the eminent architect Mr. Joseph Everett Chandler who tried to improve it as a residence in addition to preserving its old character. His book, "The Colonial House," has some information about the work.

The original house consisted of a central hall with the front half of the present staircase and with two front rooms opening off on either side of the hall on the first and second floors. The house had been erected close to the street and to the ground *(MX 3)*. The house was probably changed soon after it was erected by adding at the northwest corner a kitchen with other continuous outbuildings. One of the original chimneys stood where the entrance to the sun porch now opens in the dining room as it is now. The northeast corner had three stories of rooms which equalled in height the two main floors. This may have been built by William Drew in 1820. Mr. Chandler made extensive alterations. The house was moved back thirty feet and raised five feet. The small rooms in the rear were removed and the entire rear rebuilt with additions. The four original rooms were left much as they were. The hall was doubled in length and the original staircase was duplicated for the rear portion. The piazza was added so that persons could sit on it and see the beautiful view of Plymouth Harbor past the rock. A British coat-of-arms was placed on the roof in front as a remembrance of the Tory character of its first occupants. A magnificent organ was installed. Houses in the vicinity were demolished both to improve the view and to enlarge the garden. A gardener's cottage was built with ample space for automobiles beneath. The original kitchen was moved back and converted into an outhouse. A six foot red brick wall was built on the south and east sides of the property. It has been rumored that the expense of the project was not far from $250,000. Mrs. Willoughby was very kind and was pleased to loan the use of the house on appropriate occasions until her death in 1928. After Mr. and Mrs. Willoughby had died, their daughter and her husband lived there until the former determined to sell it, and it was placed on the market.

Many members of the Society of Mayflower Descendants had inspected and admired the house. No one appeared anxious to complete a purchase possibly for fear of the high taxes which might be increased even more. It was realized that if a patriotic society bought the house, there would be no taxes.

Among the members who were most anxious to have the Society purchase the house was little Mrs. William S. Meek from New Jersey who was loud in her advocacy that the house should be bought by the General Society and that the New Jersey Society would whole-heartedly support the raising of the money. Eventually I was informed that the owners had announced that the house was to be demolished to save taxes. It was one of the finest houses in New England of its period, and the General Society voted to purchase it for the amount of the mortgage while I was Governor General. A campaign to raise the necessary money was undertaken under the supervision of my valued co-worker Secretary-General Harold G. Murray. He deserves the greatest credit for the assistance rendered by him in the raising of the necessary funds. After these had been obtained, the General Society took title to the house on December 31, 1941. It may, therefore, be truthfully asserted that the Society of Mayflower Descendants has one of the most attractive homes in the nation. In the rear of the house is a very beautiful and extensive garden. The trees in front of the house were set out not far from 1760 by Miss Penelope Winslow, daughter of the first owner. *(R. 185)*. The house is maintained under the able supervision of our member Miss Edith S. Morissey, who is on the Executive Committee of the General Society, and a welcome is waiting there for any member who may call.

SOCIAL STATUS OF THE PILGRIMS

The question has often been asked as to the stations of life from which the Pilgrims came. Formerly and even some present day writers have described all of them as humble, uneducated folk who had no family background and were not socially equal to the Virginians or to the later Puritan settlers. Later historians have been able to uncover information formerly unknown concerning the Pilgrims, and it is now known that such statements concerning many of them are absolutely untrue.

There are several reasons why historians have concluded that the Pilgrims came from humble stock. One is because it has been impossible to identify surely the families of most of them. The cause is obvious when we realize that the Pilgrims had been fugitives whom England tried to reach even in Holland. During the long years of persecution they did not publish more than was necessary about themselves or their relatives or their homes in England. Another reason is because most of them had lowly trades in Holland. Isaac Allerton is called a tailor in the Leyden records. William Bradford was a fustian-maker. Robert Cushman and William White were wool-carders. Francis Cooke was a woolcomber. Degory Priest was a hatter. Thomas Rogers was a "camlet merchant." Samuel Fuller and Stephen Tracy were silk makers. John Jenney was a brewer *(B 39)*. Others had equally lowly occupations. The natural conclusion drawn by certain historians was that these men were humble artisans in England, but such was not the case. Many had only been used to a plain country life and the "inocente trade of husbandrey." Bradford says that when the Pilgrims went to Holland, "they were not aquainted with trads nor traffique." *(B 33)*. In Holland "they fell to such trads & imployments as they best could" so as to earn enough to keep literally from starving *(B 39)*. As fugitives in a strange country, they took any occupations which could furnish a livelihood.

Another reason is that certain historians either unintentionally or deliberately have suppressed information which shows the better social standing of the Pilgrims. For instance, certain writers say that all the Pilgrims came of yeoman stock. Since the ancestry of most of the Pilgrims is absolutely unknown, it can be appreciated that such writers are drawing on their imaginations if they mean to imply that the ancestors of all the Pilgrims were yeomen. There are, however, facts absolutely known concerning several members of the Pilgrim congregation which show that many of them belonged to the gentry.

In the days of the Pilgrims, there were certain sure indications of social superiority. Professor Morison in "Precedence at Harvard College in the 17th Century" tells about general social conditions at that time. He said that in the public records of England and also of the New England Colonies when the Pilgrims lived, a person's social station may generally be told from his title. In New England only Governors and some of the other magistrates, together with occasional sons of Knights and men who had held high position in England had Esquire placed after their names; and not all magistrates in every Colony were thus honored. Other Magistrates, Ministers, University graduates, and all others who were considered gentlemen, were designated "Mr.," and their wives and daughters, "Mrs." On formal occasions these titles were pronounced "Master" and "Mistress." Military officers were known by their military rank. These classes constituted the gentry. He added that it is an almost certain sign that a family was not considered gentle, if the head of it were not designated in the records as "Mr.," "Esq." or by some military title, at least the grade of Captain.

Norman H. Dawes, member of the Department of History at the Carnegie Institute of Technology, has written a very excellent article in the William and Mary Quarterly for January 1949, entitled "Titles as Symbols of Prestige in Seventeenth-Century New England," in which he says that prominent among the evidences of social prestige in New England were titles indicative of rank. He states that a strenuous attempt was made to maintain traditional titular honors that had long flourished in England. He finds that the titles and prefixes of respect in New England were complex. Nevertheless, clerks and recorders used titles as a means of designating the quality of an individual. He shows that there were many inconsistencies, but his comments apply to later New England and not to the period when the "Mayflower" sailed, whose passengers were addressed by titles according to English standards and not those of later New England. In England social distinctions were sharply drawn, and the social condition of each Pilgrim may be examined from the standpoint of English usage.

Hutchinson, in his "History of Massachusetts Bay," says that the first settlers were very careful that no title or appellation should be given where it was not due. Not more than a half a dozen of the principal gentlemen in the Massachusetts colony took the title of Esquire; and in a list of 100 freemen, not more than four or five were distinguished by a Mr., although they were generally men of some substance. Goodman and Goodwife were the common appellations *(H, I, 368)*.

Specifically, "Esq." was an abbreviation for Esquire. This, in theory, was the next rank above gentleman. Richer and more important gentlemen would be so designated. The head of a "County family" would be an "Esq." The sons of peers, baronets and knights would be so described if they had no other title. The Governor and certain Magistrates, Mayors, Aldermen and members of the learned professions were "Esq." The great men in the community generally were Esquires.

Bouvier's Law Dictionary states that gentleman, in English law, is a person of superior birth. "According to Coke, he is one who bears coat-armor, the grant of which adds gentility to a man's family.—In the United States this word is unknown to the law." The older dictionaries explain "gentleman" as indicating a man of good family. New English Dictionary on Historical Principles gives the primary meaning of a gentleman, as a man of gentle birth or having the same heraldic status as those of a gentle birth, properly one who is entitled to bear arms. Sir George R. Sitwell goes deeply into the matter in "The Ancestor," Vol. I, pages 58 et seq., and he concludes that primarily a gentleman was a freeman whose ancestors had always been free and from that came gradually the more modern interpretations.

"Elizabethan England" by William Harrison (L. With-

73

ington Edition, 1889), pages 7-8, was written in England in the early years of the seventeenth century. The author described a gentleman as follows:

"Whosoever studieth the laws of the realm, whoso abideth in the university (giving his mind to his book), or professeth physic and the liberal sciences, or beside his service in the room of a captain in the wars, or good counsel given at home, whereby his commonwealth is benefited, can live without manual labour and thereto is able and will bear the part, charge and countenance of a gentleman, he shall—be—reputed for a gentleman ever after—."

This means that if a man has attained a certain standard of education or accomplishment and if he does not earn his living by working with his hands and if he has the carriage, can stand the expense and has the appearance of a gentleman, he shall be thereafter considered to be a gentleman.

"Gn" is an abbreviation for "generosus," which is the Latin for "gentleman." It has also been defined as one who was well born *(BK 36)*. "Gent." was an abbreviation of "gentleman." In England "Mr." was an abbreviation for "Mister" or as it was then pronounced, "Master". "Mr." was used for more important people who occupied an important place in the community in which they lived, based in some cases on their property, in others on their education and in others on their position or office. Generally speaking, "Mr." was the same as gentleman. "The Gentility of Richard Barker" published in "The Ancestor," Vol. II, page 48, tells of a Star Chamber law case in which the issue was whether Barker's claims to being a gentleman were valid. The case is interesting as showing that being a gentleman was a matter of law and also what a Norfolk jury in 34 Henry VIII (1542/3) thought constituted a gentleman. The General Court of the Bay Colony deprived a man of his title of "Mr." as part punishment for a criminal offense. I have also found that Master was used to refer to one who had received a Master's degree or above at a College and also to refer to the employer of an apprentice. It was also used to refer to the captain and mates of a vessel.

Unmarried women of quality, as well as married women, were called "Mrs." or "Mistress." The term was applied to the wife of a "Mr." or a gentleman. It is practically the same as the title of "gentlewoman," also used.

Below the gentry, or "the quality," as they used to be called, came the great middle class of the population. The socially best of this group were termed "yeoman" or "goodman." Below this division, the people had no appellation. The yeomanry of England in the reign of Queen Elizabeth formed the class next to those who were the acknowledged gentry using coat-armor of right. (Hunter's "Founders of New Plymouth"). They formed the well-to-do farming class. "Goodman" was a respectable title used commonly but not necessarily for a farmer who did not rank as a gentleman. A servant, John Doe, would be addressed as "John," but a farmer or respectable artisan would be called "Goodman Doe." Professor Campbell's recent work, "The English Yeoman in the Tudor and Stuart Periods," is informative.

"Servant" in the 17th century did not have the modern meaning or connote necessarily a social inferiority or menial position. The term was what we today would call an employee or one who is employed by another. A servant frequently ranked only a little below the rank of his master. The term might convey that he was a companion as well as a servant. Sons of nobles took service under the King and Princes and were referred to as servants. Down the social scale, persons of every rank might have for a servant usually a person of the next lower social rank. Esquires and gentry sent their sons to serve persons of rank. When a "Mayflower" passenger is referred to as a servant, this merely means that he was an employee. A person, as now, might be employed and paid by the day, week, month, or for a year or a term of years. The contract of employment might be oral or in writing. The writing might be informal or formal. An "indentured servant" meant that the person had been bound by a formal written instrument to serve over a space of time *(AM 34/370-392)*. Such a servant might be someone who wished to be or was forced to sell his service for a period of time; in which event he would be bound during his term of service. Because one is referred to as a servant, it does not mean that he was an indentured servant. There is no evidence that any of the "Mayflower" passengers were indentured servants, and anyone so stating is drawing on his imagination. There were many so-called "servants" on the ship, and no one knows in what manner they were employed.

A civil servant, meaning a person in the civil service, remains in our speech. There is nothing menial about him. The English Common Law of master and servant is still used in this country to refer to employer and employee. Volume 39, Corpus Juris, page 33, gives the legal definition of "servant" as an "employee" as follows:

"The relation of master and servant is that which arises out of a contract of employment, expressed or implied, between a master or employer upon the one hand and a servant or employee upon the other hand."

It further states that a servant has been defined to be— "an employee." Although sometimes used in the more specific sense of a person hired to assist in domestic matters, living within the employer's house and making part of his family-hired help, the word "servant" has, in general, a broad significance embracing all persons of whatever rank or position who are in the employ and subject to the direction or control of another in any department of labor or business, and is ordinarily synonymous with "employee."

Our ancestors had definite ideas of rank, which they endeavored to enforce by legislation. Their idea of social classes was functional, as in England, rather than hereditary and genetic as in Scotland and France. A gentleman's son did not remain a gentleman if he entered a mean occupation. A gentleman might lose the title as a penalty for having committed some offense. During the times of the Pilgrims, persons were very particular not to give a title to any one to which he was not entitled.

Remembering that class distinctions at the time of the Pilgrims were well defined and that the term "gentleman" had a legal and not an ethical or cultural significance, as we now apply it, let us examine the known facts relating to the Pilgrims.

The great leader of the Pilgrims was the Rev. John Robinson. Dr. Brown, a profound student of the Pilgrims, believes him to be a son of the Rev. John Robinson, Archdeacon of Lincoln and Precentor of Lincoln Cathedral *(BR 95)*, but the Dictionary of National Biography can find no evidence to sustain this claim. Alumni Cantabrigienses states positively that the Leyden John was son of John Robinson who died at Sturston, Notts, in 1614. The Lincoln John died at Somersham in March 1597/8 so that he was another person. Our John Robinson was educated at Corpus Christi College, Cambridge, where he was afterwards a fellow. Later he became curate of St. Andrews, Norwich, where he was married. The marriage entry is "Feb. 15, 1603, Mr. John Robynson to Mistress Bridget White." He is constantly referred to as "Mr." in contemporary documents. From this fact we know that he belonged to the gentry. In 1607, he became assistant to the Rev. Richard Clyfton in the newly formed church at Scrooby, and he became sole minister of the Church at Leyden. In Leyden, he lived near the university. The following works were written by him: "A Justification of Separation from the Church of England" (1610); "Apologia Brownistarum" (1619); "Defence of the Doctrine Propounded by the Synode at Dort" (1624); "Essayes, or Observations Divine and Morall" (1625) *(B 43)*.

77

His letters show him to have been a man of education, character and ability. Nathaniel Morton called him "that famous and worthy man" (Plymouth Church Records). He was unable to sail on the "Mayflower" and died in Leyden, March 1, 1624/5 (BG) (A 5).

Their first Governor, John Carver, was the son of Robert Carver. He was baptized September 9, 1565, at Doncaster, Yorkshire, which is only seven miles from Austerfield (BK 44). He was a well-educated man, who was a leader in the religious discussions at Leyden, where he was a deacon of the church. His wife was a sister of Mrs. John Robinson. He was one of the agents of the church chosen to obtain a charter, if possible, from the king. He also negotiated with the Virginia Company for a grant of lands, and he negotiated for transportation and supplies with the Merchant Adventurers (B 52-53). His more remote ancestry is yet to be discovered, but we know that he is constantly termed "Mr." in letters written in England both before and after the coming of the "Mayflower," and that Bradford so terms him. Nathaniel Morton called him a "worthy gentleman" (Y 200) "whoe being one alsoe of a considerable estate spent the maine prte of it in this enterprise." (Plymouth Church Records). His condition in life can be seen from the fact that he and his wife brought with them on the "Mayflower" two men "servants," John Howland and Roger Wilder, also one maid servant. He was a leader among the educated men on the "Mayflower" and became the first Governor of Plymouth Colony. He obviously belonged to the gentry.

John Howland is termed a "servant" of Governor Carver. As already shown, the meaning of the word differed from its meaning at the present time and meant employee. The Governor's servant was not necessarily a person of mean social position.

John Howland was a son of Henry Howland, a prosperous yeoman, of Fen Stanton, Lancashire, England. I have in my possession a card which seems to have been printed about one hundred years or more ago, and which states the following:

"Copy from the ancient records in the Herald's College, Bennetts Hill, London. (These Arms were confirmed to Richard Howland, D.D. son & heir of John Howland of London, Gent. and allowed to him, and all the posterity of John Howland, Father of the said Richard, under the hand and seal of Robert Cooke. Clarencieux, King of Arms by patent, dated.10th June 1584, Act 27, Elizabeth.)"
Thereafter follows the Howland Coat-of-Arms after which appears the following:

"An ancient copy of this Coat of Arms is in possession of some of the descendants of Gideon White of Shelburne, Nova Scotia, whose mother was Joanna Howland, great-grand-daughter of John Howland, the Pilgrim, who came over in the 'Mayflower' in 1620."
John Howland is thought to be connected with this family, but the connection has not been definitely proved. It is significant that the coat-of-arms was used by his early descendants.

Bradford does not refer to John Howland as "Mr." but John Howland is so referred to in a letter from James Sherley, Merchant Adventurer, dated June 14, 1642, quoted in Bradford's "History" *(B 369)*. He is constantly termed "Mr." in public records. *(MD 11 70-73)*. He was a man of outstanding character, a Magistrate and one of the distinguished leaders of the Colony. Certainly he was recognized as a member of the gentry after the settlement at Plymouth. He is an ancestor of the late President Franklin D. Roosevelt.

John Howland married Elizabeth Tilley who came on the "Mayflower" with her parents, John and Elizabeth Tilley.

Of William Bradford, it is written that "he was a thoughtful, studious boy and acquired an excellent education." The Rev. Cotton Mather wrote "He had a comfortable inheritance. . . . He was a person for study as well as action; . . . he attained a notable skill in languages; the Dutch tongue was become almost a vernacular to him as the English; the French tongue he could also manage; the Latin and the Greek he had mastered; but the Hebrew he most of all studied; . . . he was also well skilled in history, in antiquity and in philosophy."

Governor Bradford was the author of the first history written in English in America. His signature is shown in R 43. He was elected Governor thirty-one times and left a library containing 275 volumes when he died. Concerning his family, the genealogist Banks shows that he was descended from Robert Bradfourth of Bentley, Parish of Arksey, County of York, England, born about 1450 and died in 1523. Robert's son, Peter Bradford of Bentley, was born about 1475 and died in 1542. His son, Robert Bradford, was born about 1500, lived in Wellingly in the Parish of Tickhill but owned land in Bentley, Arksey, Tickhill, Stansell, Wilsyke and Wadsworth, all of which were adjoining parishes, and died in 1553 *(BK 32)*. It is recorded that at the[*]subsidy of 1575, the only laymen of sufficient property to be rated at Austerfield were William Bradford, son of said Robert, and John Hanson, paternal and maternal grandfathers respectively of the future Governor. His grandfather, William, was buried in Austerfield on January 10, 1595/6. The Governor's father, William, born in 1557, was buried in Austerfield on July 15, 1591. He married Alice Hanson on June 28, 1584 *(HS II 103-110)*.

In the Parish of Bentley-cum-Arksey, there lived another Bradford family, which was armigerous (entitled to a coat-of-arms), but there is no known connection between the two families though it is possible that they had a common ancestor many generations back of the Governor's line *(BK 34)*. It is written that "from extracts of Wills and other records, we learn that the Bradfords were men of good repute and were associated with the best of

80

*See page 196.

society" *(BW 19).* Governor Bradford has been termed repeatedly "Mr.," "Gentleman," "Gent," "Gn.," and "Esq." His wife is termed "Mistris" in the Plymouth Records, and his son, Major William Bradford, was also termed "Esq." *(MD IV 25).* The social standing of Governor Bradford may be shown by his marriage because previous to the American Revolution our ancestors seldom married out of their class. His first wife, Dorothy May, is alleged to have belonged to an armigerous family in Cambridge, England. It is believed that she was probably the daughter of John and Cornelia (Bowes) May, and grand daughter of John May, Bishop of Carlisle in 1577, but this lacks confirmation *(BW 26).* In Plymouth, after the death of his first wife, the Governor married Mrs. Alice Southworth, daughter of Alexander Carpenter of Wrington, Somersetshire, England, and widow of Edward Southworth. "This lady was well-educated and brought considerable property into the country. . . . Mrs. Bradford was highly eulogized by Elder Faunce for her exertions in promoting the literary improvement and the deportment of the rising generation, according to reports which he had received from some of her contemporaries." *(T 108).*

It is claimed that the Southworths obtained their name from the Manor of Southworth in the Parish of Winwick, Lancashire, England, belonging to the Barony of Newton and through the centuries members of the family had held a distinguished position among the gentry. *(SG 405).* Governor Bradford was obviously an educated gentleman and was considered as one of the gentry.

The life of Edward Winslow was described by his friend, Nathaniel Morton, in "New England's Memorial." The following portion is taken from Rev. Thomas Prince's copy of the first edition (1669) as published in *MD IV, 1.*

"This year (1655) that Worthy and Honourable Gentleman, Mr. Edward Winslow deceased; of whom I have had occasion to make honourable mention formerly in

81

this Discourse. He was the son of Edward Winslow Esq.; of the Town of Draughtwich (Droitwich) in the County of Worcester; He travelling into the Low-Countreys, in his journeys fell into acquaintance with the Church of Leyden in Holland, unto whom he joyned, and with whom he continued until they parted to come into New England, he coming with that part that came first over, and became a very worthy and useful Instrument amongs them, both in place of Government and otherwise."

Edward Winslow and his brother Gilbert Winslow were sons of Edward Winslow, Esq., and Magdalene Olyver, his second wife. His father's first wife is said to have been Eleanor Pelham, daughter of Sir Herbert Pelham *(AM 19/534)*. The brothers were grandsons of Kenelm Winslow, Esq., of an old Worcester County family from Droitwich, England *(MD XXIX 122)*, which had existed in Worcestershire since before 1500 *(BK 98)*.

Edward Winslow was, according to Hutchinson, "of a very reputable family and of a very active genius," "a gentleman of the best family of any of the Plymouth Planters, his father, Edward Winslow, Esq., being a person of some figure at Droitwich, in Worcestershire." Winslow is said to have used a coat of arms, but the basis of his right to use it is unknown. It is, however, probable that he never would have used it had he not been entitled to it *(MD V, 224)*. It is written of Edward Winslow that "he belonged to the gentry and was an educated and accomplished man"; that he was "of high social standing" *(MD V, 224)* that his "family was ancient and honorable" *(T 90)*. He has been described as an "able and educated young English gentleman." His large estate in Marshfield was named "Careswell," after the name of an ancestral estate in Staffordshire, England. It is therefore no tradition but history that while traveling in Europe on pleasure, he visited Leyden and there became acquainted with the Rev. John Robinson and joined the Pilgrim community in 1617 *(MD XXIX*

SCROOBY CHURCH

Photographs courtesy Pilgrim Society

122). He brought two "servants", George Soule and Elias Story, with him on the "Mayflower." He served several times as Governor of Plymouth Colony and as agent both for the Colonies of Plymouth and Massachusetts Bay at the English Court. It is written that "for foreign employment his better birth and breeding gave him advantages. Among the gentlemen of the British Parliament, Winslow moved as one of themselves, and his address and winning qualities no less than his sagacity and diligence justified the choice which when he went abroad for the last time the larger Colony (Massachusetts) overlooked her own statesmen to make." Hutchison says of Winslow in England "by his prudent management, and the credit and esteem he was in with many members of Parliament and principal persons then in power he prevented any prejudice to the colony" from either of Gorton's Applications *(H I, 127)*.

Cotton Mather calls him a gentleman who was "in great favor with the greatest persons then in the nation." *(MD XXIX 122)*. While in England he published "Good News from New England" in 1624, and while there for the fourth time in 1646, he published "Hypocrisie Unmasked" and the next year "New England's Salamander." His signature appears in R 43.

There can be no question about the social standing of Edward Winslow. Some writers have seized on the fact that he made a deposition in London in 1624 calling himself "yeoman" *(BK 99)*, but this can be easily explained if one analyzes the facts. His father and grandfather being "Esq." show that his ancestry was from the gentry. Before and at the time of the sailing of the "Mayflower," he was constantly called "Mr." In 1624, when he made the deposition, he had been engaged for over three years in the most arduous kinds of manual labor on his farm in the wilderness, and he legally was then a yeoman. Later the farm became a wonderful estate, and he is again referred to as "Mr." and eventually as "Esq.," *(MD IV 12)* as his father and grandfather. Winslow, in 1654, was appointed First Commissioner by Oliver Cromwell to arbitrate and determine the value of English ships seized and detained by the King of Denmark in 1652. He was appointed by Cromwell Grand Commissioner in 1655, in charge of a British expedition against the Spanish in the West Indies, during which service he died.

Persons who know nothing concerning the social status of the Pilgrims have sought to criticize them by saying that there was no "blue blood" on the "Mayflower." Whatever "blue blood" may mean, the fact remains that the Winslows were not only outstanding in England, but the family was socially one of the best in the Colonies.

In order that the reader may understand the high position of these Winslows in the colonial society of those days, I shall describe somewhat at length the immediate ancestors of Edward Winslow, who caused the Mayflower Society house to be built. His great-grandfather was the Pilgrim Edward Winslow. His grandfather, Josiah Winslow, was born in Plymouth Colony in 1628. He was well educated and as soon as he was eligible, he was elected a member of the General Court from Marshfield. He was chosen an Assistant in 1657. In 1659, he was appointed Major or Chief Military Commander of the Colony. He was for many years a Commissioner of the Confederated Colonies. On the death of Governor Thomas Prence, he was elected Governor on March 29, 1673, and he continued to serve as such until his death on December 18, 1680. He was Commander-in-Chief of the troops raised in 1675 to defend Plymouth Colony from attacks of King Philips Indians and he commanded the English army at the Great Swamp fight in 1676. His wife was Penelope, a daughter of Herbert Pelham, Esq., a gentleman of ancient family and distinction who was graduated from Oxford in 1619 and was the first Treasurer of Harvard College. Penelope Pelham was a grand-daughter of Herbert Pelham who married Penelope

West, daughter of Thomas West, Lord De La Warr. Penelope West was descended from a sister of Queen Anne Boleyn and was of Royal descent through her mother Anne Knollys *(AG 18-138, 210)*. It has been written that "in his native colony, Governor Winslow stood on the highest ground of society. Civic honors awaited him in his earliest youth; he reached every elevation which could be attained; and there was nothing left for ambition to covet, because all had been gained. He lived on his ample paternal domain, and his hospitality was not only generous, but magnificent. In addition to his military and civic distinctions, he had acquired that of being the most accomplished gentleman, and the most delightful companions, in the colony, and the attractions of the festive and social board at Careswell were not a little heightened by the charms of his beautiful wife." *(T 139-141)*. He was greatly beloved. His piety and his social virtues endeared him to the whole colony.

His only son, Isaac Winslow, was also eminently distinguished. He was born in Marshfield in 1671 and inherited the Careswell estate of his father lying near the bounds of Duxbury and first occupied by Governor Edward Winslow as early as 1628. It was a large tract which many years later was acquired by Daniel Webster. Isaac Winslow inherited also the virtues of his ancestors, the two governors. He had a good education and devoted himself largely to public service. In his day Plymouth had become a part of Massachusetts. He had a seat in the Massachusetts House of Representatives for several years. It is said that he "was eminently distinguished, having sustained the chief places of power and honor in the colony, as chief military commander under the governor, and for several years chief Justice of the Inferior Court of Common Pleas, Judge of Probate of Wills, and one of his Majesty's Council for the Province of Massachusetts Bay for more than twenty years, and for several years President of that body." *(T 141)*. He built about 1700 the Winslow House which is still standing in Marshfield, a short distance from the site of his father's house long since gone. On July 11, 1700, he was married to Sarah Wensley, daughter of Captain John Wensley of Boston, and Elizabeth Paddy, his wife. Her father, Deacon William Paddy, was one of the most prominent of the early merchants of Plymouth and Boston. Her mother was Alice, daughter of Edmund Freeman of Sandwich. Another daughter of John Wensley, Mercy, married Joseph Bridgham of Boston and was the grandmother of Mercy Bridgham, wife of Dr. William Thomas, who is mentioned herein.

Isaac Winslow was much given to hospitality and was universally beloved. He died at his home in Marshfield on September 7, 1738, leaving several children.

His eldest son, a young gentleman of great promise, by the name of Josiah, engaged in military service, received a captain's commission, and was killed in battle, with thirteen of his company, after a most gallant resistance against a superior force of French and Indians in 1724. General John Winslow, the eldest of the surviving sons of Isaac, was a distinguished and successful commander. In 1740, he commanded a company in the expedition against Cuba, and afterwards rose to the rank of Major General in the British service. In 1755, an expedition against Nova Scotia was undertaken by the British government, of which General Monckton was commander-in-chief, and General (then Colonel) John Winslow, second in command. So great was the popularity of Colonel Winslow, that in an incredible short time he raised for this expedition two thousand men. The two French forts were captured with scarcely any loss on the part of the conquerors, and the whole Province completely reduced, chiefly through the enterprise and good conduct of Colonel Winslow; to him too was entrusted the difficult and delicate task of removing the French neutrals. In 1756, (as General and Commander-in-chief of Provincial troops), he commanded at Fort William Henry, on Lake George. *(T 142-143)*. In 1757, he was commissioned to be Major General in the King's service and in 1759, he acted as such in the expeditions against Canada. He served as President of the Old Colony Club in 1769. He was also a counsellor of the Province. He died at Marshfield in 1774, at the age of seventy-three years.

I have already described the excellent social standing of Edward Winslow, builder of the old house. The foregoing record of these Winslows amply proves that there was a "blue blooded" family on the "Mayflower" and there were others.

George Soule is believed to be the son of John Soule of Eckington County, Worcester, England, and probably kinsman to Robert Soule, a wealthy London salter, who died in 1590, a native of Eckington *(BK 80)*. His autograph is in existence *(MD IV 98) (R 43)*.

Myles Standish was a professional soldier who had served in Holland as an officer in the English Army. Nathaniel Morton was born in Leyden in 1613 and was in a position to obtain first-hand information concerning him. In his "New England Memorial" he says of Standish, "He was a gentleman, born in Lancashire and was heir apparent unto a great estate of lands and livings, surreptitiously detained from him." The historian, Rev. William Hubbard, wrote before the close of the 17th century that he "was allied to the noble house of Standish, in Lancashire, inheriting some of the virtues of that honorable family as well as the name. His family dated back to 1222, and in his will he mentioned a claim to lands to which he was entitled by descent in seven localities." *(MD III, 153-156)*. His American estate was in Duxbury, and he assumed the arms and crest of the English Standishes of Duxbury in England. His statements in his will identify him as a member of the Ormskirk branch of the Standish family in Lancashire *(BK 82) (Wilson's Chorley Church)*. That branch of the family held lands as described in the will *(SA 344)*. He is referred to as "gent" and obviously belonged to the English landed gentry.

Samuel Fuller was a physician who has been described as "eminent in his profession, devoutly pious and wise in counsel in the affairs of the Colony." Edward Fuller was his brother. It is claimed in "New Light on the Pilgrim Story" that they were sons of Nicholas Fuller of Stepney who was a barrister admitted to Grays Inn in 1587 and who became Treasurer of the Inn in 1591 and in 1601 a member of Parliament, but this book seems to be wrong in this regard. It seems proved beyond question that the father was Robert Fuller, a butcher *(FE) (FS)*.

The father is elsewhere called Robert Fuller, a "yeoman." Irrespective of his father's occupation, Bradford terms Samuel Fuller "Mr." *(B 407-411)*. He brought a "servant" William Butten with him on the "Mayflower" and was a distinguished surgeon and physician *(B 302)* whose fame extended over New England. When the first Puritan contingent arrived at Salem, there was much sickness and many died. Hearing of the reputation of Dr. Fuller, the Salem settlers asked Governor Bradford to permit him to come to Salem which request was granted. In a letter of thanks to Bradford from John Endicott, dated May 11, 1629, the latter said "I acknowledge my selfe much bound to you for your kind love and care in sending Mr. Fuller among us." *(B 260)*. Dr. Fuller was obviously considered a member of the gentry. His letters in Governor Bradford's Letter Book show that he was a well educated man *(M.D. VII 79-82)*. His signature is shown in R 43.

Richard Warren was a merchant of London. He is spoken of as "a man of some means and of superior character; such a man as would be a valuable acquisition to any company about to found a new commonwealth." The author of "New Light on the Pilgrim Story" believes him to have been connected with Sir Ralph Warren of the Mercer's company and a close relative of Oliver Cromwell, but no proof of this is furnished. Dr. John Collins Warren, M.D., in "Genealogy of Warrens with Historical Sketches," published in Boston in 1854, mistakenly identifies him with Richard Warren, son of Christopher and Alice (Webb) Warren of Headborough, England. The 1620 Herald's "Visitation of Devonshire" states that Richard, son of Christopher, was then a merchant of Greenwich, Kent. This line shows a descent from William, Earl of Warenne and Surrey, who accompanied and married the daughter of William the Conqueror. The Harleian Society Publication of "Visitation of Devonshire" in 1620, page 354, shows that Dr. Warren's line does not refer to Richard Warren of the "Mayflower" but to another Richard Warren who was a merchant in Greenwich, Kent, and who married the widow Elizabeth (Jouatt or Ivatt) March or Marsh. This last Richard had two sons, Richard Warren and John Warren. This demolishes the Royal line prepared by Dr. Warren because the children of Pilgrim Richard Warren were Mary, Anna, Sarah, Elizabeth, Abigail, Nathaniel and Joseph. This other Richard Warren was baptized in England at Sydenham Damrell on August 15, 1619, and was five years younger than his wife, Mrs. Elizabeth March or Marsh, who was not licensed to marry her first husband until August 20, 1629. This first marriage of Elizabeth was one year after Pilgrim Richard Warren had died at Plymouth. So he could not have been the Richard who married her at a time when he was dead. The matter is clearly explained in Roebling's "Richard Warren of the Mayflower" on pages 4 and 5 also by other authorities including Charles Browning in his errata to "Americans of Royal Descent." A suggestion has been made that Richard Warren of the "Mayflower" was the person who was Sheriff of Coventry in 1610 (HX II 21). It has been impossible to identify the ancestors of Richard Warren of the "Mayffower." (BK 92). The fact remains that the Norman de Warren or Warren family is one of the oldest and best in England. We know that Bradford and others refer to Richard Warren constantly as "Mr." *(B 408, 412)*. Nathaniel Morton in his "New England's Memorial" likewise mentions him as such. These contemporary references show that he was considered as belonging to the gentry. He is an ancestor of former President Ulysses S. Grant while the late President Franklin D. Roosevelt is descended from him in five lines.

Richard More was not a waif picked up in the streets of London as has been erroneously alleged in "The Mayflower and Her Log." His family pedigree has been traced at length and is published in Volume 36 of the New York Genealogical and Biographical Record, page 213, et seq. This account shows that he was descended from the distinguished English County family of More in Shipton, County Salop, England, which family was entitled "to bear coat armor," which means to have a coat of arms. The first of the family is believed to have been Richard de la More, who accompanied William the Conqueror in the Norman invasion. The Pilgrim Richard More was the son of an outstanding man, Samuel More of Shipton, who was born in 1594, and was called the "Parliamentarian." The father is described as "Generosus," that is to say he was well born. His father married his third cousin Katherine More of Larden on February 4, 1610-1611. The latter was a daughter of Jasper More of Larden, who can be traced back eight generations to William More of Shipton. The family is described in Burke's "Landed Gentry," Edition 1898, Vol. I, page 1059. The Pilgrim Richard More was baptized at Shipton, on November 13, 1614. One brother and his sisters are also mentioned in the Shipton parish register. *(MD V, 256) (BK 72)*.

The most active Merchant Adventurer connected with the sailing of the "Mayflower" was Mr. Thomas Weston, a merchant of London. Bradford in his history mentions him at length. He had been baptized in 1583 in Hughby, Shropshire, which is three miles from the Shipton Church section and Larden Hall, where the Mores lived, and he undoubtedly was an old friend of the More family. It was, therefore, natural that Richard More was living with Thomas Weston in London before embarking on the "Mayflower." In Plymouth, Richard More became a member of the family of William Brewster. He did not change his name to Mann or Man *(MD III, 192-201)*, as has been erroneously alleged. Richard Man of Scituate was an entirely different person who was drowned in early 1650. Richard More died a respected resident of Salem on March 19, 1693/4 (OS) or March 29, 1694 (NS), and his resting place has the only original gravestone (of a Pilgrim) in existence.

Of Isaac Allerton it is said, "He was admittedly the first merchant of New England, and the founder of the coasting trade and the fishing industry." In the parish of Saint Andrew Undershaft, an Allerton family lived to whom Isaac may have been related. *(BK 14)*. All efforts to trace his exact ancestry in England have been unavailing, but there can be no question about his being considered as one of the gentry. In 1614, he had the honor of being admitted as a burgess of Leyden in Holland. He represented the Pilgrims in England in negotiating with the Merchant Adventurers. Bradford says that he was selected as the agent of the colonists as "being well qualified by education and experience, and having the confidence of the Merchants of London." Bradford and others constantly refer to him as "Mr." *(B 407, 410)*. He brought a "servant," John Hooke, with him on the "Mayflower." He was elected the first Assistant to the Governor in 1621 and served in that capacity for many years. He represented the Colonists in England and at the English Court where it is said "he obtained the love and favor of great men in repute and place; he got granted from the Earl of Warwick and Sir Ferdinando Gorges, all that Mr. Winslow desired." *(MD VII 7) (B 249)*. His selection as one to associate with nobility does not indicate mean birth. In New Amsterdam he is termed "Mr." in the records where he was a member of the Council of Eight to assist the Governor. He was obviously a man of the greatest ability and distinction. He is an ancestor of former Presidents Zachary Taylor and of Franklin D. Roosevelt. His autograph is in existence *(MD XXV 97)* *(R 43)*.

Their Elder William Brewster was of gentle birth *(MD IV 102)*. Brewsters lived from earliest times in the Scrooby region and in the neighboring parishes of Yorkshire. In 2 Richard II (1379) there was a Robert Brewster in Bawtry which adjoins Scrooby. A William Brewster was taxed in Bentley-cum-Arksey in 1524 who could be the grandfather of 'Elder' William. *(BK 35)*. His father's official position as steward and bailiff of the Manor of Scrooby gave the son a recognized social standing when he attended Peterhouse, Cambridge University *(BK 36)*. Later he was for sometime assistant to Queen Elizabeth's Secretary of State, Sir William Davison. Bradford in his history described William Brewster at length as follows: "After he had attained some learning, viz. the knowledge of the Latine tongue, and some insight in the Greeke and spent some small time at Cambridge, and then being first seasoned with the seeds of grace and vertue, he went to the courts, and served that religious and Godly gentleman, Mr. Davison, diverce years, when he was Secretary of State; who found him so discreete and faithful as he trusted him above all other that were aboute him, and only employed in all matters of the greatest trust and secrecy" *(B 376) (Y 463)*. Bradford goes on to say that Davison esteemed Brewster rather as a son than as one working for him; because of Brewster's wisdom and godliness, Davison, in private, would converse with him more like a friend and companion than an employee. Bradford tells how Brewster attended Davison when the latter was sent by Queen Elizabeth as an Ambassador to the Low Countries in the Earl of Leicester's time. When the keys of Flushing were delivered to Davison in her Majesty's name, he kept them sometime, after which he handed them to Brewster who kept them under the pillow on which he slept the first night. Before Davison's return to England, the Dutch authorities honored him with a gold chain which he handed to Brewster and commanded him to wear it when they arrived in England and rode through the country, until they reached the court. Brewster remained with Davison until the latter lost his position because of the death of Mary Queen of Scots. *(B 377)*. Hunter in "The Founders of New Plymouth" says that Brewster must have been a man of some position by birth to have obtained appointment in Davison's service. Brewster returned home on leaving Davison's service and, on the death of his father a year later, became Postmaster of Scrooby. This was a very responsible position in those days because the letters sent by post usually, if not always, were government missives. Personal correspondence went by private hand. Of this period of his life Bradford said, "Afterwards he wente and lived in the country, in good esteeme, amongst his freinds and the gentlemen of those parts." *(B 377)*. It was in his home in the old Manor at Scrooby that the Pilgrim Separatists met in secret communion.

Hunter in his "The Founders of New Plymouth" described Brewster's home as a great manor place, standing within a moat, and belonging to the Archbishop of York. He further said that it had belonged to the see of York in the time of Domesday Book and that the Archbishop not unfrequently resided there. On June 12, 1503, Margaret, queen of Scotland, daughter of King Henry VII, slept there on her way home. When Wolsey was dismissed by King Henry VIII and sent to his northern diocese, he passed some weeks at Scrooby. It is interesting to note that King Henry VIII slept there for one night during his northern progress in 1541. Arbishop Sandys, who was elevated to the see of York in 1576, leased the Manor to his eldest son Samuel, and it must have been under him that the Brewsters held the Manor.

William Brewster was an educated gentleman, who at first taught English to students in the University in Leyden and afterwards engaged in publishing books proscribed in England. Among these were "Commentarii in Proverbia Salomonis" (1617) by Thomas Cartwright with a preface by Polyander; an abridgment of a reply by William Ames to "Grevinchovius on the Arminian controversy" (1617); "A Confutation of the Rhemist's Translation of the New Testament" (1618) by Thomas Cartwright; a treatise in Latin "De Vera et Genuina Jesu Christi Religione" (1618) and other works. His signature is shown in R 43. He preached in Plymouth from 1620 to 1629 in the absence of the Rev. John Robinson. While living in his house in Plymouth, which was built by his own hands, he yearly received supplies of newly published books in Latin and English, and his library was inventoried at his death at 400 volumes. *(MD IV 102; III 19-27)*. In the Proceedings of the Massachusetts Historical Society, 2nd Series, Volume V, pages 37-85, may be found a paper prepared by Rev. Henry M. Dexter concerning these books. He studied Hebrew when quite an old man as a help to his understanding of the Bible. "But what especially distinguished him as a religious leader in those days was his breadth, toleration and charity. When that sturdy and heroic heretic, Roger William, in Plymouth denounced the Mother Church in England as Anti-Christ, pronouncing it sinful to attend its worship or to fellowship with it, the more charitable Leader of the Pilgrims refused to go with him or to hold to any such nonsense." "The claim that the Elder was in the slightest degree blameworthy in advising the Plymouth Church to accept Roger Williams' petition for a dismissal from that church to the church in Salem will hardly pass muster with any student of history thoroughly conversant with the 'chip on the shoulder' characteristics of the great Founder of

Rhode Island, or who has thoughtfully read Bradford's words of tender regret at the parting — words which undoubtedly echoed the sentiments of the Elder." *(MD IV, 106, 107)*.

The officials of the High Court of Commission, who summoned him for religious contumacy in 1607, addressed him as "William Bruster of Scrowbie gent" *(BK 36)*. In the list of freemen entered in 1636 at Plymouth, "Gn" appears after his name. He is constantly termed "gentleman" *(BR 98) (MD III 27)*, also "Mr." *(B 407, 410) (MD I, 9)*, and obviously belonged to the English gentry. He is an ancestor of President Zachary Taylor.

There has been no record found which can be surely identified as the marriage of William Brewster, but some historians believe that the evidence supports the fact that he married in 1591 at Scrooby, Mary Wentworth, daughter of Thomas Wentworth, who was the predecessor of William Brewster's father at Scrooby Manor. The Wentworth Genealogy, Edition 1878, which has been approved for its accuracy, lists Mary Wentworth and shows that her father was Thomas Wentworth, son of Sir Thomas Wentworth, who was knighted for bravery at the Battle of Spurs in 1513. The latter was called "Golden Thomas." He paid a fine in order to be excused from accepting the Order of the Bath. In 1528, he obtained a license from Henry VIII to remain covered in the royal presence because of his health. This Wentworth family is traced in the Wentworth Genealogy back to Rynold, Lord de Wynterwade, (the old way of spelling Wenthworth) of Yorkshire, who was living at the time of William the Conqueror. A Wentworth first cousin of this Mary Wentworth had a grandson, Sir Thomas Wentworth, Baronet, who became Baron and Viscount Wentworth, Baron of Raby and Earl of Strafford. He was beheaded May 12, 1641, during the troubles between Charles I and Parliament.

Degory Priest, like Bradford and Allerton, had the honor

of having citizenship of Leyden conferred on him. His ancestry is unknown, though his name was common in Devon and Cornwall *(BK 75)*. He married a sister of Isaac Allerton.

Christopher Martin was an outstanding Pilgrim. His ancestry is unknown. He is referred to by Bradford as "Mr. Martin from Billirike in Essexe" *(B 76)*, but the records there do not give us the answer. He seems to have been an able business man who helped in the preparations for the voyage of the "Mayflower." Bradford and others refer to him constantly as "Mr." *(B 76, 408, 411)*. Bradford states that he was Governor of the ship during the voyage. He brought two servants, Solomon Prower, who was a son of his wife by a previous marriage *(BK 70, 76)*, and John Langemore *(MD I, 9)*. He obviously belonged to the gentry.

William Mullins (Mullines or Molines) is thought by some to have been a Walloon, who had taken his residence in Dorking, County Surrey, England. It is claimed that he was a representative in the eighteenth generation descended from Robert Molyneaux, Comte de Moulin *(AM 19/542)*. This is denied by Ames in "The Mayflower and Her Log." His ancestry has really never been traced. He seems to have been a man of some wealth. He occupied an estate in the Manor of Dorking which he bought in 1612. *(BK 73)*. He is described in Morton's "Memorial" as "a man pious and well deserving, endowed also with a considerable outward estate; and had it been the will of God that he had survived, might have proved a useful instrument in his place" *(Y 181)*. He brought a servant, Robert Carter, on the "Mayflower." His will, written by Governor Carver and witnessed by him and by Dr. Giles Heale, surgeon of the "Mayflower," and by Captain Christopher Jones, shows that he held nine shares in the Adventurers Company *(MD I, 230-232)*; see also *(MD XXXIV, 1-7)*; *N.E. Hist. Gen. Reg., Vol. 42, page 62; Proceedings Mass. Hist Society, 2nd Series, Vol. 5, page 38)*. He is termed "Mr." by Bradford *B 82, 408, 411)* and was obviously one of the gentry. Through his daughter Priscilla, who married John Alden, he is an ancestor of Presidents John Adams and of John Quincy Adams.

John Alden, who later became son-in-law of Mr. Mullins, was "hired for a cooper" at Southampton and was not a member of the Pilgrim community before the sailing of the "Mayflower." His ancestry has never been traced. An Alden family resided in Harwich, County Essex, England, at that time and was related by marriage to Captain Christopher Jones. One of this family, named John Alden, was possibly the Pilgrim *(BK 28)*. He may have been related to Robert Alden, one of the merchant adventurers. The tradition surrounding his marriage to Priscilla Mullins is described in Longfellow's "The Courtship of Myles Standish." He became an Assistant, served as Deputy Governor and was an outstanding member of the Plymouth community. He wrote an excellent autograph *(MD VII 1) (MD XXV 145) (R 43)*. While Bradford does not term him "Mr." in his list of passengers, he does so term him in his history *(B 363)*. He is also so termed in the Plymouth Colony records. Governor Thomas Dudley of Massachusetts Bay Colony terms him "Mr." in a letter dated May 22, 1634 *(B 306, 307)*. James Sherley, one of the merchant adventurers, terms him "Mr." in a letter dated 14 June 1642 *(B 369)*, and he is constantly termed "Mr.", "Gent" and finally "Esq." in contemporaneous records. Whatever may have been his family, he was considered a member of the gentry after the arrival of the "Mayflower." He is likewise an ancestor of Presidents John Adams and John Quincy Adams.

In "New Light on the Pilgrim Story," it is claimed that William White, who married Dr. Samuel Fuller's sister[*] Susanna, was a son of the distinguished John White, D.D., of Oxford, rector of Barham, near Ipswich, Suffolk, England, and Chaplain to King James the First, but I have found nothing to sustain this claim. It is said that in his will he mentioned his son William who had left his Church

*See page 196.

and his Country. Mrs. Haxtun agrees with this contention. *(HX I 26)*. Banks doubts the descent because he could not locate where the son William had been so mentioned *(BK 94-95)*. If the descent is true, our William was a great nephew of Sir Thomas White, Lord Mayor of London.

Our William White was a first cousin of Governor Carver's wife. He is termed "Mr." by Bradford *(B 408-411)* and brought two "servants," William Holbeck and Edward Thomson, with him on the "Mayflower" William White obviously belonged to the gentry. His son Peregrine, born on the "Mayflower" was also later termed "Mr." *(MD III 119)*.

It has been frequently alleged that Thomas Rogers was a descendant of the Martyr the Reverend John Rogers, prebendary of St. Paul who was burned alive at Smithfield in the presence of his wife and children by order of Queen Mary. This has been asserted in "New Light on the Pilgrim Story" and in other books *(HS I 131)*. Other authorities are not prepared to accept the line and claim that it has not been proved. Until further convincing evidence is found, the line should not be considered as proved. Bradford does not refer to Thomas Rogers as "Mr." *(B 408, 412)*.

"New Light on the Pilgrim Story" alleges that Francis Cooke was a grandson of Sir Anthony Cooke, which statement is shown to be quite untrue by Banks. Banks offers evidence that he, as well as his wife Hester Mahieux might have been a Walloon *(BK 48) (MD VIII 48)*. Mr. Bowman says that he is English *(MD III 95)*. Haxtun claims he came from Blyth, a parish adjoining Austerfield from a family which had manorial rights *(HX II 3)*. He seems to have been a person of respectability. Bradford does not refer to him as "Mr." *(B 408, 412)*. He is an ancestor of President William Howard Taft, and President Franklin D. Roosevelt is descended from him twice.

Stephen Hopkins was one of the outstanding persons on the "Mayflower." Lefroy's "Memorials of the Bermudas" tells how he had been a lay reader with Governor Sir Thomas Gates of Virginia when the latter sailed in the "Sea Adventure" from England to Virginia in 1609 and was wrecked in Bermuda *(BK 61-62) (NE XXXIII, 305)*. Returning to England, after a stay in Virginia, Stephen Hopkins came back to America on the "Mayflower." Some writers claim that he was a great-grandson of Stephen Hopkins, fellow and Professor in Kings College, 1532, and Rector of Norfolk, England, 1551, and that his parents were Nicholas Hopkins and Mary Poole, sister of Sir Giles Poole *(HS I, 116)*. Though one of the more prominent Pilgrim congregation, his exact ancestry has not been positively identified. A Stephen Hopkins family lived in Saint Katherine Coleman Parish, London, and our Stephen married his second wife only a short distance away *(BK 14)* so that he may be related to this family. Bradford says that he came from London *(MD V, 47)*. He brought two "servants," Edward Doty and Edward Leister, with him on the "Mayflower." Bradford terms him "Mr." *(B 408, 411)* and he is called "Mr." and "Gn" in the Plymouth records. Obviously, he was considered as belonging to the gentry.

Both Edward Doty and Edward Leister signed the Mayflower Compact *(MD XXII 59)*. Haxtun claims that Edward Doty (Dotey) (Doughty) was an English youth belonging to the same family as Sir Charles Montague Doughty or Doty of Therburton Hall, Suffolk County, England, formerly of Lincoln County. She says that this family dated back to the Norman Conquest. Being a minor Edward Doty came over in the employ of Stephen Hopkins *(HX II 32)*. This line needs more substantiation.

Henry Samson came, when a young boy, from Saint Andrew Undershaft, London, from where Isaac Allerton also came. He came with Edward and Ann Tilley, being called their "counsin" by Bradford *(B 408)*. He was a proprietor, freeman and volunteer in the Pequot War. He seems to have become a person of standing, but absolutely nothing is known concerning his forbears.

It has been alleged that Peter Brown was descended from Sir Thomas Browne (*HS 131-133*), but this line may not be accepted without further proof.

James Chilton was a citizen and tailor of Canterbury in 1583. His father, Lyonel Chilton, or as the father signed his name, Lyonell Chylton, was referred to as yeoman and was a person of considerable property in the Parish of St. Paul, Canterbury. He was a church warden of St. Paul from 1578 to 1579 as was his son John later. The father's will was made on September 7, 1582, and was proved in the Archdeaconry Court of Canterbury on February 13, 1582/3. In the will the father left money to charity and lands with buildings to his sons John and James. The estate left to James was called "Wullsack." Lyonel's wife Isabel, mentioned in the will, was a second wife and was not the mother of his children. She was the widow of Francis Furner and had not been long married when the will was made. The grandfather of James Chilton was Richard Chilton, or as the grandfather signed his name, Rycharde Chilton, who also lived in the Parish of St. Paul, Canterbury. The grandfather's will dated September 21, 1549, was proved in the Archdeaconry Court of Canterbury on November 30, 1549. The grandfather refers to his late wife Isabell. After arranging for certain payments to the poor, he mentions three servants. The grandfather left all his remaining property to his son Lyonel Chilton, father of the Pilgrim, James Chilton.

The church register of St. Paul, Canterbury, records the baptism of two of James Chilton's children. He moved to the parish of St. Martin where two other children were born and two others died. He later lived in the parish of St. Peters, Sandwich, where two more children were born (*BK 45*). While he is not termed "Mr." by Bradford (*B 408, 413*), his daughter, Mary, married "Mr." John Winslow

(MD II 116; III 133) and is termed "Mrs." Her son is also termed "Mr." *(MD I, 67, 71)*.

I have described at length the leaders of the Pilgrims. Many of the other passengers on the "Mayflower" were their wives and children. Certain of the others were their servants and laborers. As already shown, many of the Pilgrims undoubtedly came of "gentle blood." While we do not know whether the ones we cannot trace came of "gentle blood," yet this fact we know, an extraordinary number of the Pilgrim men, including many whom we cannot trace, obviously belonged to the gentry and in the gentry were included those of "gentle blood." If one compares the list of the Pilgrims with the lists of any other migration to the Colonies, one will be impressed by the larger proportion of Pilgrim men who obviously belonged to the gentry.

It has been stated that "The Swiss republic was an aristocracy of birth, and the Dutch republic an aristocracy of wealth. Our English yeomen and artisans could not have founded the one or the other; but the twelve leaders who were distinguished among their fellows by the then significant title of 'master' would have been commended by the best English and Continental sentiment of their day if they claimed official and social superiority. Their nobility showed itself in anticipating the day when 'just and equal laws', adopted and administered by the people, should govern great nations." *(G 63)*.

The magistrates of Leyden said that the English had lived amongst them ten years "and yet we never had any suit or accusation against them." *(M 12-13)*.

William Hilton, who came on the "Fortune," wrote a letter to England dated November 1621 in which he said:

"Our company are, for most part, very religious, honest people; the word of God sincerely taught us every Sabbath; so that I know not anything a contented mind can here want." *(Y 251)*.

The historian Brown says: "The story of the Pilgrims

101

has all the elements of a fascinating romance. When it is read in the light of what they have produced and in the spirit of sympathy which appreciates and enjoys the religious and civil liberty we inherit, it is fitted beyond most uninspired records, to kindle exalted ideas of citizenship and to stimulate young and old to self denying service of our country and of mankind." *(BR V)*.

The secret of Pilgrim character may be found in the words of Bradford which give his explanation as to why they succeeded: "What could now sustaine them but the spirite of God and his grace?" *(B 97)*. Elsewhere he said: "Such was the true piety, the humble zeal and fervent love of this people towards God and his ways, and the single heartedness and the sincere affection one towards another, that they came as near the primitive pattern of the first Churches as any other church of these later times have done according to their rank and quality" *(MD IV, 11)*. "By God's assistance they prevailed and got the victorie" *(B 38)*. And elsewhere he said: "May not and ought not the children of these fathers rightly say: 'Our fathers were Englishmen which came over this great ocean and were ready to perish in this willdernes, but they cried unto the Lord, and he heard their voyce, and looked on their adversitie, etc. Let them therefore praise the Lord, because he is good, and his mercies endure forever. Yea, let them which have*re- deemed of the Lord, show how he hath delivered them from the hand of the oppressour. When they wandered in ye deserte willdernes out of ye way, and found no citie to dwell in, both hungrie, & thirstie, their sowle was overwhelmed in them. Let them confess before the Lord his loving kindnes, and his wonderfull works before the sons of men'." *(B 97)*.

There have been in the history of the world many examples of persons who have placed their trust in God and were inspired by faith to attain what was apparently unattainable. With success seemingly impossible, these persons

102

overcame terrifying and apparently insurmountable obstacles by an inspiration derived from a belief that God would answer their prayers and that their efforts would therefore end in victory. They had complete confidence that God was personally helping them. If God is with them, they did not see how anything could succeed against them. The Pilgrims lived exalted lives. By reading the Bible and by prayer, they were convinced that they were in communion with God and that nothing could defeat them. Nothing did. One of the greatest arguments for the power of prayer is the example of those persons, like the Pilgrims, who with sublime faith place their complete trust in a loving God and thereafter succeed in overcoming every obstacle. If any person of a succeeding generation gets discouraged and begins to lose hope, let him read the story of the Pilgrims who trusted in the promises made in the Bible and who showed succeeding generations what faith will accomplish for those who put it to the test.

I have described at length much of what is known about the Pilgrims so that people generally may appreciate the real truth concerning them. The Pilgrim men and women left a record of which the world is justly proud. Theodore Roosevelt well summed up when he said: "The coming of the Pilgrims to these shores, three centuries ago, shaped the destinies of this Continent, and, therefore, profoundly affected the destiny of the whole world." Their descendants and all other Americans have a duty to carry on the Pilgrim tradition by maintaining the Pilgrim's standards in their lives and by being their worthy successors. In the words of Thomas Carlyle, "Hail to thee, poor little ship Mayflower of Delft Haven; poor, common-looking ship; hired by common charter-party for coined dollars; caulked with mere oakum and tar; provisioned with vulgarist biscuit and bacon; yet what ship argo or miraculous epic ship, built by the sea gods, was other than a foolish bumbarge in comparison." And in the words of the Rev. Minot J. Savage, "I would rather claim my descent from one of the Pilgrim group than from any other source in the world. No other great name, no nobleman, no King, could tempt me for a moment as to ancestry if I could be proud enough to point back to the Mayflower."

Let us finally remember what the late Dean LeBaron Russell Briggs said at the end of his remarkable poem delivered at the 1920 celebration;

"The Pilgrim's faith, the Pilgrim's courage grant us;
Still shines the truth that for the Pilgrims shone.
We are his seed; nor life nor death shall daunt us.
The port is Freedom! Pilgrim heart, sail on!"

APPENDIX A

This is a list of those who came over on the "Mayflower," as listed by Governor Bradford, with some additional information by me concerning their lives. All dates are in the new style. *(B 407-414)* (George Ernest Bowman, "Mayflower Compact and Its Signers with a List of the Mayflower Passengers," Boston, 1920).

In some instances Bradford has spelled the name of the person differently from the spelling which appears in Morton's list of signers and which is believed to be correct by the historians. In such cases I have used when possible, the spelling which is considered to be a copy of an original signature.

Bradford gave to certain of the men the designation of "Mr." I have done the same. This should be pronounced *master.*

In referring to the employees, called servants by Bradford, I have not used the word "indentured." Bradford did not use it when describing any passengers on the "Mayflower." No other source record has it. "Indentured" means a written document whereby a contract is made, and an indentured servant might be bound for any time, even for a term of years. There is no evidence which indicates whether the employees on the ship were employed orally or in writing, and if in writing, whether informally by memorandum or by the more formal indenture. I have, therefore, not referred to the employees on the "Mayflower" as being indentured because it would be an unwarranted conclusion which has no factual basis.

1—*John Alden* was born about 1599 *(MD II 114) (MD III 121).* According to Bradford, he was "hired for a cooper at South-Hampton, wher the ship victuled; and being a hop-full yong, man, was much desired, but left to his owne liking to go or stay when he came here; but he stayed, and maryed here." *(B 409)*. His duties as cooper were to care for the casks of salt meat, beer and water. He was the seventh signer of the Mayflower Compact. Bradford continues:" Mr. Molines, and his wife, his sone, and his servant dyed the first winter. Only his daughter Priscila survied, and maried with John Alden, who are both living, and have 11 children." *(B 411)*. His marriage to Priscilla Mullins at Plymouth must have been before 1624. It is poetically described in Longfellow's "The Courtship of Myles Standish." In "Early American Furniture Makers" by Thomas H. Ormsbee, it is alleged that Alden was the first trained woodworker in any English speaking colony on the American continent. The author says that Alden was sometimes referred to as a "joyner," which means that he did cabinet work and furniture making in addition to his office holding, farming and trading with the Indians. None of the furniture made by him is extant. He resided at first in Plymouth where he owned a considerable tract of land. About 1632, or perhaps earlier he moved to Duxbury, where he had 169 acres of land in one parcel, and there he passed the rest of his life. He was in Captain Myles Standish's Duxbury Company in 1643. In 1653, he built there the house that is still standing. He was always active in the affairs of the Colony. In July, 1627, he was one of the undertakers who became responsible for the debt of the Colony. *(B 227-229)*. In 1634, he had gone to carry supplies to the trading post on the Kennebec River in Maine. He did not even witness the justifiable killing in self-defense of John Hocking there by one of John Howland's men, yet he was arrested and imprisoned when he later stopped in Boston. *(NE IX 80) (Maine Hist. Coll. 3, 2, 322)* Standish procured his release. *(B 306)*. On October 15, 1641, he entered into contract with James Sherley and the other Merchant Adventurers, on behalf of the Colony *(B 359-362)*.

The business with Sherley was finally settled on June 14, 1642 *(B 368-371)*. He was an Assistant from 1632 to 1640, 1650, 1686. He was a Deputy to the General Court, 1641, 1642, 1644, 1649. He was a Member of the Council of War, 1646, et seq. He was Acting Deputy Governor, 1644, 1677. After the death of Captain Standish, he was for some time Treasurer of the Colony. Thacher describes him as follows: "He possessed much native talent, was decided, ardent, resolute, and persevering, indifferent to danger, a bold and hardy man, stern, austere and unyielding, of exemplary piety, and of incorruptible integrity" *(T 156)*. "He hated innovations and changes, steadily walked in the ways of his youth, and adhered to the principles and habits of those whom he had been taught to honor." His wife died after 1650 *(MD II 114)*. When he died at Duxbury on September 22, 1687, *(MD II 114)* he was the last surviving signer of the Compact. He left no will *(Plymouth County Probate Records, Vol. I, pp. 10, 16)*. John Alden has had many descendants who, in addition to Presidents John Adams and John Quincy Adams, include Henry Adams, Charles Francis Adams, Arthur Adams, and other members of this very distinguished Adams family. Other descendants have been Samuel Seabury, first Episcopal Bishop in America; Judge Joshua Thomas, first President of the Pilgrim Society; Governor Jonathan Trumbull of Connecticut; William Cullen Bryant, the poet; Henry Wadsworth Longfellow, author of "The Courtship of Myles Standish"; Charles Stratton, better known as General Tom Thumb; Ambassador Charlemagne Tower; Artemas Ward, benefactor of Harvard; James Bryant Conant, President of Harvard; Charles H. Stone, the engineer; Congressman Robert Low Bacon; Mrs. Henry L. Stimson; Actress Betty Field; Theatrical Producer Vinton Freedley; George Albert Smith, late head of the Latter Day Saints or Mormon Church; and many more who are equally distinguished.

2—*Mr. Isaac Allerton* came with his wife, three children

and one servant *(B 407)*. He is credited to the Leyden group and was the fifth signer of the Mayflower Compact. He was born about 1586 *(MD IV 128) (BK 29)*. He married, first at Leyden on November 4, 1611, Mary Norris of Newbury, County Berkshire, England *(NE 15, 30-31)*. His sister married Degory Priest also on November 4, 1611. In 1614, he was admitted as a burgess of Leyden. When the "Mayflower" sailed, he had four possibly five children, all born in Holland, three of whom came over with their parents on the "Mayflower." His daughter, Sarah, remained behind and came over with her aunt Sarah Priest. He was awarded a garden plot in Plymouth, but in 1635 he was living at Rockynook, on Jones River, Kingston.

In April, 1621, after Governor Carver died, William Bradford was chosen governor and Isaac Allerton was chosen sole Assistant to the Governor or Deputy Governor, a position he held until 1624. In September, 1621, he was one of a party of ten which explored the harbor of Boston at which time the first headland at Nantasket was named Point Allerton. His wife having died at Plymouth on March 7, 1621, in the first general sickness, he married, second, at Plymouth, between July 1623 and June 1, 1627, Fear Brewster, daughter of the Elder, who had come in the ship "Ann" in 1623 with her sister Patience. She died at Plymouth on December 12, 1634.

He was an Assistant from 1624 to 1631, and also in 1633. In the fall of 1626, Isaac Allerton was sent by the colonists to England. In the spring of 1627 he returned with a proposed contract by which a group of persons composed of William Bradford, and several others including himself, assumed the entire indebtedness of the colony. He was at once sent back to England to close it. He returned to Plymouth, and during the next few years he crossed the ocean seven times. James Sherley wrote of him on March 8, 1629, "He hath been a truly honest friend to you all, either there or here. And if any do, as I know some of them are apt to

108

speak ill of him, believe them not." And again on March 19, 1629, he wrote, in a letter signed also by Timothy Heatherly, a friend of the colonists in London, "But the Lord so blessed his labours (even beyond expectation in these evil days), as he obtained the love and favor of great men in repute and place, he got granted all Mr. Winslow desired in his letters to me and more also." It was soon after this that he had controversies with Bradford who claimed that Allerton sometimes endeavored to favor his own interest rather than those of the colony. In 1629, Allerton employed the notorious Thomas Morton, as his secretary, which gave so great offense that he was obliged to dismiss him *(T 71)*. He was admittedly the first merchant of New England, and the founder of the coasting trade and fishing industry. He accompanied Governor Bradford and Dr. Fuller to Salem in July, 1629, to assist in the ordination of Mr. Skelton and Mr. Higginson. He then ranked first in wealth among the colonists *(T 71)*. He was the first to welcome Winthrop and his company on June 12, 1630, when they arrived in America at Charlestown. In 1632, he tried to set up a rival trading station on the Kennebec, also on the Penobscot, but they were unsuccessful. In 1633, he had a fishing fleet off Marblehead where he was staying with his son-in-law. His character may be inferred from the following passage quoted from the Old Colony Records "1633 desb'r 2d. Whereas Mr. Will. Bradford was appointed in the behalfe of the Court to enter upon the estate of Godbert Godbertson and Zarah his wife, and to discharge the debts of the said Godbert so far as his estate will make good. And whereas the greatest part of his debts are owing to Mr. Isaack Allerton of Plymouth merchant late brother of said Zarah, the said Isaak hath given free leave to all other his creditors to be fully discharged before he receive any thing of his particular debts to himself desiring rather to lose all than other men should lose any" *(T 71-72) (OCR I 20)*.

In 1634, many misfortunes came to him, including the

death of his wife on December 12th. His misfortunes still
continued, and he eventually was notified to leave Marble-
head. From 1636 to 1646 he resided most of the time at New
Amsterdam where he was engaged in the coasting and
tobacco trades. He went into partnership with Governor
Loockermans, and in 1643 was one of the eight men of
New Netherland. In 1647, he purchased a tract of land and
built a warehouse and residence where Peck Slip now is.
He married, third, before 1644, Joanna who survived him
(MD II 114). He was often in New Haven after leaving
Plymouth and became a resident there as early as 1646,
although retaining his business and residence at New Amsterdam. He died at New Haven between the 10th and 22nd
of February, 1659, and is supposed to have been buried on
the New Haven "Green." His New Haven residence from
1646 to 1659 was on Fair Street and is marked by a tablet
(HS II 175). His will has been published *(MD II 155) (New
Haven Probate Records, Vol. I, part 1, pgs. 82, 83)*. He has
had many descendants *(AH) (I) (MI) (HS 173-182, 183-187)*,
only a few of whom can be mentioned.

His son Isaac moved to Virginia, married and had a
daughter Sarah who became the second wife of Hancock
Lee, son of Col. Richard Lee, founder of the very distin-
guished Lee family. Their daughter Elizabeth Lee married
Zachary Taylor, and they were the parents of Lt. Colonel
Richard Taylor of Revolutionary fame. The last had a son
Zachary Taylor who became President of the United States.
The last was the father of Lt. General Richard Taylor,
C.S.A. in the Civil War and Sarah Knox Taylor, first wife
of Jefferson Davis, President of the Confederacy. Hancock
Lee and his wife Sarah Allerton had a son Hancock Lee,
who was father of Willis Lee and Captain Hancock Lee,
who were among the first explorers of Kentucky with their
cousin Hancock Taylor, killed there by the Indians in 1774.
Other distinguished descendants of this line include Col.
Francis Taylor of the Virginia Line in the Continental

Army; Brig. General Joseph Pannell Taylor, U. S. Army in the Civil War; Major General George Bibb, C. S. Army, Civil War; Major General Thomas Leonidas Crittenden, U. S. Army, Civil War, whose son Lieutenant John Crittenden, 20th U. S. Infantry, was killed by Indians at the Battle of Little Big Horn; also the Rev. William C. Young, President of Centre College. Isaac Allerton's blood is in many of the most outstanding families in Virginia, as well as elsewhere. As already shown herein, another descendant is the late Franklin Delano Roosevelt, four times President of the United States.

3—*Mary (Norris) Allerton* was from Newbury, County Berks, England. She came with her husband and three children *(B 407)* and died in the general sickness on March 7, 1621 *(MD VII 129-130) (R 210) BK 29).*

4—*Bartholomew Allerton,* son of Isaac by his first wife Mary Norris, was born at Leyden, Holland, about 1612. *(HX 16).* He came with his parents on the "Mayflower." He was too young to sign the Mayflower Compact. He was a resident of Plymouth in 1627, but shortly afterwards he accompanied his father to London where he became a minister, married and had children. He never returned to America and, so far as is known, no descendant of his has ever been found in this country. A chancery suit of 1657, in which Bartholomew Allerton was a defendant, relates to property in Suffolk, the parties being residents of Norfolk. He was mentioned as clerk of "Bamfield" (probably Bramfield), County Suffolk, when his will was proved in 1659. He mentions late wife Margaret, present wife Sarah and his children without naming them *(BK 30) (MD II 114).*

5—*Remember Allerton,* daughter of Isaac Allerton, by his first wife Mary Norris, was born at Leyden, Holland, about 1614. She came with her parents on the "Mayflower" and was living at first in Plymouth. Later she married about 1633, and certainly before May 6, 1635, Moses Maverick, Pastor, *(MD V 129) (HS II 178-179)* and lived in Marblehead, which was originally a part of Salem. She died at Salem between September 12, 1652, and October 22, 1656. Her husband, Moses Maverick, married, second, at Boston on October 22, 1656, Eunice (Cole) Roberts, widow of Thomas Roberts *(HS II 179)*. He died at Marblehead, February 7, 1686 *(MD II 114-115)*.

Many have been misled by an article in the New England Historical and Genealogical Register *(VII 265)* in which the author stated without quoting any authority that Moses Maverick married Sarah Allerton and that Remember probably died unmarried and without issue. This was published before Bradford's History was discovered *(B 411) (MD V 130)*. "The Allerton Family, 1585-1885," page 49, copied the mistake. In the Essex County Registry of Probate at Salem is a record that the Maverick children are from "Moses and Rember Maverick."

6—*Mary Allerton,* daughter of Isaac and Mary (Norris) Allerton, came with her parents and with her brother and sister. She was born in Leyden, Holland, in June, 1616. She married at Plymouth about 1636, Thomas Cushman, son of Robert Cushman, who was born in February, 1608, and who had come with his father in the "Fortune" in 1621. In Plymouth he had been brought up in the family of Governor Bradford. He was chosen Ruling Elder of the Church in 1649, after the death of Elder Brewster. He died at Plymouth, December 21, 1691. A tombstone was erected to his memory in 1715, by the Church and congregation at Plymouth *(T 67)*. She died at Plymouth, December 8, 1699, and was the last survivor of the "Mayflower" passengers *(MD II 115)*. She has left descendants *(MI)*.

7—*John Allerton* was a seaman hired to be one of the company that was to go back for help of others behind *(B 409)*. He was the thirty-eighth signer of the Mayflower Compact. He took part in the third expedition which left the "Mayflower" on December 16, 1620, in the shallop to find a suitable place for a permanent settlement. He thereafter took part in the First Encounter with the Indians and later landed and assisted in selecting Plymouth as the place for the permanent settlement *(MR 43) (B 9).* He died at Plymouth during the general sickness between January 11 and Aplrl 10, 1621 *(MD II 115).* He is not known to be related to Isaac Allerton. He left no descendants.

8—*John Billington* came with his wife and two sons from London *(B 408).* He was the twenty-sixth signer of the Mayflower Compact. He was the first offender to be punished. In 1621, John Billington was charged with contempt of the captain's lawful command and of opprobrious speeches. He was tried by the whole company and sentenced to have his neck and heels tied together; but, on humbling himself and craving pardon, and it being his first offense, he was released from his painful situation before the time had expired *(T 37).* In 1625, Governor Bradford said to Robert Cushman in a letter, "Billington still rails against you, and threatens to arrest you, I know not wherefore. He is a knave and so will live and die *(T 72).* He eventually was executed for murder at Plymouth in September, 1630. Bradford describes his passing as follows: "This year John Billington the elder (one who came over with the first) was arrained, and both by grand and petie jurie found guilty of willful murder, by plaine and notorious evidence. And was for the same accordingly executed. This, as it was the first execution amongst them, so was it a mater of great sadnes unto them. They used all due means about his triall, and tooke the advice of Mr. Winthrop and other the ablest gentlemen in the Bay of Massachusetts, that were then newly come over, who concured with them that he ought to dye, and the land be purged from blood. He and some of his had been often punished for miscariags before, being one of the profanest families amongst them. They came from London, and I know not by what freinds shufled into their company. His facte was, that he way-laid a yongman, one John New-comin (about a former quarell) and shote him with a gune, whereof he dyed" *(B 270-271)*. He has had many descendants.

9—*Eleanor Billington,* wife of John came with him and their two sons *(B 408)*. They were married before 1605. She was accused of slandering Deacon John Doane and sentenced to a fine of five pounds and "to sit in the stocks and be publickly whipt" *(HS I 57)*. She survived her husband, married, second, at Plymouth in September, 1638, Gregory Armstrong. Eleanor died after March 12, 1643. Her second husband died at Plymouth, November 15, 1650 *(MD II 115)*.

10—*John Billington,* eldest son of John and Eleanor, came with his parents and brother Francis *(B 408)*. He was born before 1605 but was too young to sign the Mayflower Compact. In July of 1621 he was lost in the woods. Inquiry was made, and Massasoit sent word that he was at Nauset. He had wandered about five days, subsisting on berries. The governor sent ten men in a shallop, with the Indians Squanto and Tockamahamon, to recover him *(B 118-119)*. The party was obliged to take shelter from a storm in Commaquid (Barnstable) harbor. They sent Squanto to the Sachem Aspinet who was accompanied by not less than one hundred warriors when he brought John back. Half of these warriors went to the shallop unarmed, carrying John through the water, while the rest remained at a distance carrying their bows and arrows. John returned to Plymouth with the Plymouth men *(T 40-41))*. John Billington, Jr., died at Plymouth between June 1, 1627, and September, 1630 *(MD II 115)*. He never married.

11—*Francis Billington* came with his parents and brother John *(B 408)*. He was born about 1606 and was too young to sign the Mayflower Compact. He nearly blew up the "Mayflower" *(MR 42-43)*. About January 1, 1621, he mounted the top of a tree on a high hill and announced that he had discovered in the distance another great sea. A week later he went with one of the master's mates to have a view of the place. They found the water divided into two lakes; the large one had five or six miles compass, the smaller one had three miles *(T 31)*. Thereafter the larger was known as Billington Sea. He married at Plymouth in July, 1634, Christian (Penn) Eaton, widow of Francis Eaton. She died at Middleborough about 1684. They seemed to have ill fortune because they were forced to bind out most of their children to secure means for their existence. Francis was occasionally sued and fined and once had the choice of a whipping or paying twenty pounds. In later life he did better and served on committees, etc. *(HX II 26)*. He died at Middleborough, December 13, 1684 *(MD II 115)*. He has had many descendants.

12—*Mr. William Bradford,* son of William and Alice (Hanson) Bradford, came with his wife Dorothy (May) Bradford. They left their son behind *(B 407)*. William Bradford was the second signer of the Mayflower Compact. Any account of him means giving a history of the Pilgrim movement. The town of Gainsborough in Lincolnshire, and the villages of Austerfield and Bawtry in Yorkshire, and Scrooby and Babworth in Nottinghamshire were on or near what was once called the great North Road. Many Separatists lived in these localities. Bradford was born in Austerfield where he was baptized on March 19, 1590 *(AM 19/522)*. After a long sickness, when about twelve years of age, he became deeply impressed by the preaching of the Rev. Richard Clyfton at Babworth. Bradford had been in the care of uncles from the time his parents died when he was about two years of age. These uncles remonstrated with him because they knew that the consequences of joining the Separatists might be confiscation of all property, banishment or death. His answer, written while a boy, shows the character and nature of his entire life:

"Were I like to endanger my life or consume my estate by any ungodly courses, your counsels to me were very seasonable. But you know that I have been diligent and provident in my calling, and not only desirous to augment what I have, but also to enjoy it in your company, to part from which will be as great a cross as can befall me. Nevertheless, to keep a good conscience and walk in such a Way as God has prescribed in his Word, is a thing which I must prefer before you all, and above life itself. Wherefore, since it is for a good Cause that I am likely to suffer the disasters which you lay before me, you have no cause to be either angry with me or sorry for me. Yea, I am not only willing to part with everything that is dear to me in this world for this Cause, but I am thankful that God hath given me a heart so to do, and will accept me to suffer for him" *(B 6)*.

When it was decided by the members of the Scrooby group to remove to Holland, Bradford, then aged about seventeen years, was ready to go. After many difficulties he reached Amsterdam in 1608 and moved to Leyden in 1609. In Amsterdam he had been employed by a Frenchman in the working of silks. When he came of age in 1611, he was able to convert his inheritance into money. In Leyden he was in the business of making fustian, a type of cloth like corduroy. On November 30, 1613, he was married to Dorothy May of Wisbeach, Cambridgeshire, England *(B 8)*. By the time the group left Holland for America, he was one of their leaders (Mass. Hist. Soc. Proceedings, Vol. 61, pp. 34-40, 55-58). On the arrival of the "Mayflower" in Cape Cod Harbor on November 21, 1620, an expedition was fitted out to explore the land to which he was one of the men added as counsel *(MR 13-14) (B 8)*. It was shortly thereafter that he was caught in an Indian deer trap made with a noose attached to a bent twig *(B 9)*. He also possibly took part in the second expedition by persons whose names have not been recorded. He was a member of the third expedition which had the First Encounter with the Indians and which landed and selected Plymouth as a settlement *(MR 43)*. When he returned to the "Mayflower" on December 22, he learned of the death of his wife Dorothy by accidental drowning on December 17, 1620 *(MD XXIX 98, 118)*.

An interesting contemporary document bears evidence of the severity of the first winter. Thomas White of Dorchester, writing in 1630, to a friend in England, asserts that when the settlers landed at Plymouth ten years before, there was a foot of snow on the ground *(B 9)*. When Governor Carver died about the middle of April 1621, Bradford was chosen to succeed him and served every year thereafter until 1657, with the exception of 1633, 1636 and 1644 when Edward Winslow served and 1634 and 1638 when Thomas Prence served. He also served as an Assistant, 1634, et seq. He married, second, at Plymouth on August 24, 1623, Alice, daughter of Alexander Carpenter and widow of Edward Southworth who came on the "Ann" in July of that year. His "History of Plymouth Plantation" is a classic. His other literary productions are outstanding. Cotton Mather says of his death, "at length he fell into an indisposition of body which rendered him unhealthy for a whole winter (1656-1657), and as Spring advanced his health yet more declined . . . He died lamented by all the Colonies of New England as a common blessing and Father to them all" *(B 3-19)*. He died at Plymouth, May 19, 1657 *(YAI) (HS II 105)*. His will has been published *(MD II 228)* (Plymouth Colony Wills and Inventories, Vol. II, part 1, pgs. 53-59). He was probably buried on Burial Hill; so in 1835 a gravestone was placed for him by the known grave of his son William who, tradition said, had expressed a wish during his lifetime to be buried next his father. Bradford's widow died at Plymouth on April 5th or 6th, 1670 *(MD II 115)* *(AM 19/527)*. He left many descendants *(BD) (BW) (MI)*, of whom I mention a few. William Bradford was followed by his very distinguished son, Deputy Governor Major William Bradford. Persons of the Bradford name have continued to be prominent. Among them have been Gamaliel Bradford, Colonel in the Revolution; William Bradford, first U.S. Senator from Rhode Island; Alden Bradford, early Secretary of State of Massachusetts; Governor Robert Bradford of Massachusetts; and author Roark Bradford. Among other descendants have been the late Dean Le Baron Russell Briggs, president of Radcliffe College; James Bryant Conant, President of Harvard; Charles Seymour, President of Yale; Arthur Coolidge, Lt. Governor of Massachusetts; the late John Pierpont Morgan, banker; the Right Reverend James DeWolf Perry, Presiding Bishop of the Episcopal Church; Wilbur L. Cross, Governor of Connecticut; Harold Eugene Edgerton, Professor of M.I.T. and noted inventor; Carl R. Gray, President of the Union Pacific Railroad; General Carl R. Gray, Jr., head of the Veterans' Administration; and Major General "Jimmy" Doolittle. Among the distinguished women descendants are Mrs. Alexis I. duPont and Mrs. Louisa Pierpont Satterlee.

13—*Dorothy (May) Bradford* came with her husband William, leaving their son John behind *(B 407)*. John had been born in Leyden. He came over later and lived at various times in Duxbury, Marshfield and Norwich, in which latter place he died childless in 1678 *(BW 77)*.

Dorothy May was born about 1597. She married William Bradford at Amsterdam, Holland, on December 9, 1613, *(AM 522) (HX 5)*. She was accidentally drowned at Cape Cod Harbor on December 17, 1620 *(MD II 115) (MD XXIX 98, 118) (MD XXIII 24)*. The first allegation that she committed suicide was contained in a fictional and imaginative account published by Mrs. Jane Austin in Harper's New Monthly Magazine in June, 1869. This authoress did not pretend to be accurate in her historical stories. To use an old saying, she "never let the truth spoil a good story." Any publication which repeats as fact the absolutely unfounded story of Mrs. Austin's may be rightfully considered as historically unreliable in its statement.

14—*Mr. William Brewster,* who was born about 1566/7 *(BM I 3) (MD II 115) (DN 253, 273)*, came with his wife

Mary and his two sons Love and Wrestling *(B 407)*. He was the fourth signer of the Mayflower Compact. He probably had much to do with the preparation of this document. The rest of his children were left behind and came over afterwards. He attended Peterhouse College, Cambridge University, from about 1580 to 1583 *(HS II 27)*. That year he entered the service of Sir William Davison, then Ambassador to Holland. After the latter lost his position, Brewster obtained the appointment of the Post at Scrooby, a position previously held by his father. He kept this position from April 1, 1594, to September 30, 1607, when he was in trouble because of his religious activities *(B 5)*. He married before 1593 *(MD II 115)* a wife Mary who has been tentatively identified as Mary Wentworth, the daughter of his predecessor in the Scrooby post.

Brewster had been pious from his youth and was early found among those who opposed the ceremonies and forms of the English Church. Those who wished to leave the Established Church, known as Separatists, met in groups in private houses, and one group met in his Scrooby home. Eventually persecution drove its members to flee secretly to Holland in 1607 and 1608. When the members of the Scrooby group were arrested for trying to escape from England, all except seven were discharged after one month's confinement. He was among the seven who were kept in prison *(B 34)* and, therefore, was one of the last to escape to Holland *(B 38)*. At Amsterdam where they resided for a year and at Leyden, where they settled for over ten years more, Brewster taught the English language. He also engaged in the business of printing prohibited religious books and introducing them into England by stealth from about 1616 to about 1619. During the latter years he was under cover, seeking to avoid arrest by the English authorities. He, together with John Carver and Robert Cushman, conducted the negotiations for the emigration to America *(B 8)*. He was long the ruling Elder of the Church, and in

Plymouth he conducted all services for many years because Robinson stayed in Leyden and there was no ordained minister in Plymouth. After the death of James Chilton, he was the oldest of the Pilgrims. He was one of those leaders who assumed the debt of the Colony *(B 227-229)*, and who settled with Merchant Adventurer Sherley *(B 371)*. A deputy to the General Court in 1636, he also was Chaplain of the Military Company. He died at Plymouth, April 20, 1644 *(MD II 115) (MD I 7) (BL X 1) (MD III 15)* (Plymouth Col. Wills, Vol. I, pg. 53) (Court Orders, Vol. II, pg. 101). Bradford's description of him is touching *(B 375-382)*. One of the most remarkable characters that this county has ever had, he has had many descendants *(BM) (MI)* of whom I mention a few.

William Brewster shares with his son-in-law Isaac Allerton the credit of being the ancestor of many of the most distinguished residents of Virginia. Sarah Allerton, who married Hancock Lee, was a great grand-daughter of William Brewster, so the latter is ancestor of Elizabeth Lee, who married Zachary Taylor and became the ancestor of President Zachary Taylor, whose daughter Sarah Knox Taylor was the first wife of Jefferson Davis, President of the Confederacy. I shall not repeat the other distinguished persons in this line mentioned under the Allerton head; they include some of the best blood in the South. Among other descendants are Benjamin Brewster, Bishop of Maine; Owen Brewster, U. S. Senator from Maine; Henry Wadsworth Longfellow, the poet; Major General Amiel Weeks Whipple, early American explorer of the Southwest; Robert Low Bacon, former Congressman; James W. Wadsworth, Jr., former U. S. Senator from New York and Congressman; and Winthrop Aldrich, the banker. Among the distinguished women descended from him are the late Mrs. John D. Rockefeller, Jr., sister of Mr. Aldrich, also the first Mrs. Albert Conway, wife of the Associate Justice of the New York Court of Appeals.

15—*Mary (tentatively identified as Wentworth) Brewster* came with her husband and two sons *(B 407)*. She died at Plymouth on April 27, 1627 *(MD II 115)*.

16—*Love Brewster* came with his parents and brother Wrestling *(B 407)*. He was born about 1611 and was too young to sign the Mayflower Compact. He married at Plymouth on May 25, 1634, Sarah Collier, daughter of Merchant Adventurer William Collier. She was born about 1615. Love Brewster was admitted a freeman of Plymouth Colony on March 2, 1635/6. He early moved from Plymouth to Duxbury. In 1637, his name appears among those who volunteered to serve in the Pequot War. He was a member of Capt. Myles Standish's Duxbury company in the military enrollment of 1643. In 1645, he was a proprietor of Bridgewater. He died at Duxbury in January or February, 1651. *(MD I 162)* *(MD II 115, 203)* (Plymouth Colony Wills and Inventories, Vol. I, fols. 89-91). His widow married, second, after September 1, 1656, Richard Parks of Cambridge, Massachusetts, who died there between July 12 and October 19, 1665 *(MD II 115)*. Sarah returned to Duxbury after Parks' death and was living there March 12, 1679/80. She died at Plymouth May 6, 1691 *(B 27)*. Love Brewster has had many descendants.

17—*Wrestling Brewster* came with his parents and brother Love Brewster *(B 407)*. He was too young to sign the Mayflower Compact. He died unmarried between June 1, 1627 and August 1643 *(MD II 115)*.

18—*Richard Britteridge* came alone *(B 409)*. He was the thirty-fourth signer of the Mayflower Compact. He was probably from London *(BK 40)*. His was the first Plymouth death. He died without known issue while the "Mayflower" was in Plymouth Harbor, December 31, 1620 *(MD II 115)*, "in the general sickness that befell" *(B 413)*.

19—*Peter Brown* was from Great Burstead, Essex, England. He came alone *(B 409)*. He was the thirty-third signer of the Mayflower Compact. He was a brother of John

Browne, the weaver *(BK 41)*. On January 12, 1621, with John Goodman, he was gathering thatch when they came to a lake of water (probably Murdock's pond). Their two dogs found a fine large deer and chased it. They followed until they were lost. They wandered all night in the frost and snow without weapons or food. In the night they were alarmed by noises which they supposed to be the roaring of lions. They mounted a tree for safety with intervals of walking beneath it. At early dawn they renewed their wanderings, and it was not until night that they reached the settlement. Later they learned that what they thought were lions were really wolves *(MR 73-74) (T 31)*. Peter Brown married first at Plymouth in 1624 or 1625 Mrs. Martha (   ) Ford who had come on the "Ann" and who died at Plymouth between June 1, 1627 and 1631. After her death, he married, second, between 1627 and 1631, Mary   , who died at Plymouth after January 12, 1634 *(MD II 115-116)*. Brown was registered among the early settlers of Duxbury as a freeman. He was fined for not being at the General Court on January 1, 1633 *(HX II 27) (PCR I 5)*. He died at Plymouth about September, 1633. His estate has been listed *(MD V 29) (MD I 79) (HS II 132)*. He is said to have had "divers children by divers wives" *(MI)*, but Bradford says he married twice and had two children by each wife *(B 413)*.

20—*William Butten* came as a servant to Samuel Fuller. He was a son of Robert Butten of Austerfield, England, and was baptized in the Austerfield Church on February 12, 1598, O.S. *(B 94, note)*. Bradford says of him, "In all this viage ther died but one of the passengers, which was William Butten, a youth, servant to Samuell Fuller, when they drew near the coast." *(B 94)*. He died on November 16, 1620 *(MD II 116) (B 17)*. He left no descendants.

21—*Robert Carter* came over as a servant of William Mullins. He did not sign the Mayflower Compact, perhaps because he was not free to do so or because he did not intend to remain permanently. He probably came from London or vicinity. In the will of William Mullins, the testator asks that his executors "have a special eye to my man Robert weh[*]hathe not so approved himself as I would he should have don." *(BK 43) (HS II 214).* He died without issue at Plymouth in the general sickness after March 3rd, 1621 *(MD II 116).*

22—*Mr. John Carver* came with his wife, Catherine, Desire Minter, two men servants (John Howland and Roger Wilder), a maid servant and a boy (William Latham). Jasper More accompanied him *(B 407).* He was the first signer of the Mayflower Compact. He is believed to have been a son of Robert Carver and to have been baptized September 9, 1565, at Doncaster, Yorkshire, England, which is approximately seven miles away from Austerfield and next to Bentley, where other Pilgrim families like the Brewsters and Bradfords had resided. He married Mrs. Catherine (White) Leggatt, widow of George Leggatt, who was the daughter of Alexander White of Sturton-le-Steeple in Nottinghamshire about 1608 *(BG 22).* Her sister Bridget has been previously referred to as the wife of the Rev. John Robinson at Leyden *(BK 44).* Carver was elected first Governor of the Colony before landing *(B 10, 107-116)* and served as such only four months and twenty-four days. He was a man of great prudence, integrity and firmness of mind. He had a good estate in England, which he spent in the migration to Holland and America. Piety, humility and benevolence were eminent traits in his character. He took part in the third expedition from the "Mayflower" in the shallop which had the First Encounter with the Indians where is now Eastham and which made the permanent landing at Plymouth *(MR 43).* He conducted the making of the treaty with Massasoit *(B 10, 11).* Both before and after the arrival of the "Mayflower," he acted as agent for the Pilgrims *(B 8, 52, etc.).* He signed the will of Williams Mullins as a witness. At the time of the general sickness

*See page 196.

he was assiduous in attending to the sick after his own recovery. On April 5, 1621, he was taken sick in the field while engaged in planting and died in a few days *(B 116) (T 37-38)*. His wife died at Plymouth five or six weeks after her husband in May, 1621 *(MD II 116) (BK 44)*. They left no known descendants.

23—*Catherine (White) Carver* was the daughter of Alexander White of Sturton-le-Steeple, Nottinghamshire. She first married George Leggatt. After his death she married John Carver *(BK 44) (HS II 128)* and died at Plymouth in May, 1621, five or six weeks after her husband *(MD II 116)*.

24—   , maid servant of Mrs. John Carver. Bradford says "His maid servant married and dyed a year or tow after, here in this place" *(B 410)*. She probably married Francis Eaton *(MD II 116)*. Her name is unknown.

25—*James Chilton* was born probably about 1563 *(HS II 101)*. He came with his wife and daughter Mary *(B 408)*. He was the twenty-fourth signer of the Mayflower Compact. He was a citizen and tailor of Canterbury in 1583 and was active in the affairs of the Merchant Adventurers. He first was in the parish of St. Paul and later St. Martin of that city. He later lived in St. Peter's parish, Sandwich, where several of the Pilgrims lived prior to their moving to Leyden. He died on the "Mayflower" at Cape Cod Harbor on December 18, 1620. His wife died after January 11, 1621 *(MD II 116) (AM 19/543)*. He has had descendants *(MI)*, including Mrs. James A. Garfield, wife of the former president of the United States and her sons James R. Garfield, former Secretary of the Interior, Harry A. Garfield, late President of Williams College; Irvin A. Garfield, the architect; and McDowell Garfield, the lawyer.

26—   (   ) *Chilton,* wife of James Chilton, died in the first general sickness sometimes after January 11, 1621 *(MD II 116) (BK 45)*. Her unmarried name is unknown.

27—*Mary Chilton* was probably born about 1608 *(BK 45)*. She married at Plymouth between July, 1623 and June 1, 1627, John Winslow, who was born at Droitwich, England, April 26, 1597. He was brother to Edward Winslow. He arrived on the "Fortune" in 1621. They first resided at Plymouth *(AM 19/543-544)*. In Pilgrim Hall is a certificate of their dismissal from the Plymouth Church to the Boston Church. He moved to Boston in 1655 and became a prosperous shipping merchant. He died at Boston, Massachusetts, between March 22 and May 31, 1674. She died there shortly before May 11, 1679 *(MD II 116)*. "Mary Chilton's Title to Celebrity," by Charles Thornton Libby (privately printed, Boston, 1926) tells about the tradition that she was the first to land. Her will has been published *(MD I 65)* (Suffolk County Registry of Probate, VI, 300-301). A copy of the inventory is in Probate Records, XII, 314-15. She is buried with her husband in King's Chapel Burying Ground next to the later grave of Paul Revere. She has had many descendants.

28—*Richard Clarke* came alone *(B 409)*. He was the thirty-sixth signer of the Mayflower Compact. He died during the general sickness sometime between January 11 and April 10, 1621 *(MD II 116) (B 413)*. Many have claimed descent from him, but the Society of Mayflower Descendants has not allowed their claims.

29—*Francis Cooke* came with his son John. His wife and other children came afterwards on the "Ann" *(B 408)*. He was the seventeenth signer of the Mayflower Compact. He was living in Leyden seven or eight years before the arrival of Robinson and the remainder of the Pilgrims which leads one to believe that he had no prior association with the Pilgrim group. He is recorded as "Franchois Couck" in the Leyden records which give his betrothal date of June 9, 1603. His bride Hester Mahieu described as spinster from Canterbury in England, and his two witnesses were all Walloons *(BK 48)*. There was a large group of Walloons in Canterbury *(HS I 156)*. This furnishes an uncertainty as to whether he was originally English or Walloon. He was married on July 20, 1603, in Leyden, Holland *(MD XXVII 145-155)* *(MD VIII 48)*. Francis Cooke settled at Rocky Nook, now in Kingston. He was made a freeman in 1633. In 1634, he was a referee in settlement of various affairs between members of the Colony, and he was thereafter employed by the community in various capacities. From 1637 to 1647 he was a juryman. In August, 1643, he was listed as able to bear arms. In 1662, he was one of the proprietors of Dartmouth (now New Bedford) but never lived there *(HX II 5)*. He died at Plymouth on April 17, 1663. His will has been published *(HS I 157)*. (Plymouth Col. Wills and Invent., Vol. II, Part II, folios 1, 2). His widow died after June 18, 1666, and before December 28, 1675 *(MD II 116)*. He has had many descendants *(C) (MI)* who include Alphonso Taft, Ambassador to Russia; William Howard Taft, President of the United States, and Charles Taft, U. S. Senator. Other distinguished descendants are Franklin Delano Roosevelt, President of the United States, Major General Leonard Wood, Commander of the Rough Riders and later of our armies in Cuba during the Spanish American War; Charles Allerton Coolidge, architect who built the college houses at Harvard; Charles Dudley Warner and many others.

30—*John Cooke* came with his father. His mother with other children came afterward *(B 408)*. He was baptized at Leyden between January 1 and March 31, 1607 *(MD XXVII 153)*. He married at Plymouth on April 7, 1634, Sarah, daughter of Richard Warren. In 1637, he volunteered for service in the Pequot War. From 1640 to 1653 he was a juryman. In August, 1643, he was listed as able to bear arms. He was Deputy to the General Court from 1638 to 1656 from Plymouth and he served in 1666, 1668, 1675, 1679, 1682 and 1686 from Dartmouth, where he settled. He also served as Deacon *(HS II 6)*. He built the ferry between Dartmouth and Rhode Island. He became a Quaker and later a Baptist preacher. He died at Dartmouth December 3, 1695, and was buried at Oxford, Fair Haven. His will and inventory are on file (Bristol Co. Probate Records I, 139-140). His widow died after July 25, 1696 *(MD II 116)*. They have had many descendants.

31—*Humility Cooper* came in the family of Mr. and Mrs. Edward Tilley. Bradford describes her as their cousin *(B 408)*. She was probably from London. She had one acre granted to her in 1623 adjoining that of Henry Samson, who was also related to the Edward Tilleys *(BK 49)*. She later was sent for and returned to England and died there *(B 412)* between 1627 and 1651 *(MD II 116)*. She has left no known descendants.

32—*John Crackston* came with his son John, Jr. *(B 407)*. He was the twenty-fifth signer of the Mayflower Compact. He was one of the Leyden contingent and is supposed to have come from Colchester, County Essex. Davis thinks the name of Crackston's wife was Smith *(BK 50)*. He died in the first mortality *(B 411)* between January 11 and April 10, 1621 *(MD II 116)*, possibly the first part of March. He left a daughter Ann, at Leyden, who married Thomas Smith, a wool carder, from Bury St. Edmunds, England *(HX II 21)*. No descendants are known to have lived in the United States.

33—*John* [2] *Crackston* came with his father of the same name *(B 407)*. Bradford says "John Crackston dyed in the first mortality; and about 5 or 6 years after, his sone dyed; having lost him selfe in the wodes, his feet became frosen, which put him into a feavor, of which he dyed." *(B 411)*. The date was 1627 *(MD II 116)*. He left no descendants.

34—*Edward Doty* was of London. He came as a servant, perhaps meaning employee, of Stephen Hopkins *(B 408)*. He was the fortieth signer of the Mayflower Compact *(HX II 32)*. He apparently married Wynifryd Waryner, December 12, 1613, at St. Mary-le-Strand, London *(BK 51)*. He came without his wife. On December 16, 1620, he left with the third expedition from the "Mayflower" in the shallop which resulted in the first encounter at Eastham two days later and in the first landing at Plymouth *(MR 43)*. He was given one allotment after landing, which shows that he was alone at the time. On June 18, 1621, he was arraigned with Edward Leister before the company for trial because they had fought a duel with sword and dagger in which both were wounded. They were sentenced to have their heads and feet tied together and to remain in the situation for twenty-four hours without food or drink. The punishment was remitted by the governor after one hour's endurance in consequence of their pleadings and promises and the earnest desire of their employer Mr. Hopkins *(T 38)*. He married, second, at Plymouth, on January 16, 1635, Faith Clark, and died at Plymouth on September 2, 1655 *(MD III 87)*. His will has been published *(HS II 139-140)* (Plymouth Colony Wills, Vol. II, part 1, pg. 14-16). His widow married, second, on March 14, 1667, John Phillips, who was born about 1602 and died at Marshfield, between October 30, 1691, and May 19, 1692. His wife, then Mrs. Phillips, died and was buried at Marshfield on December 31, 1675 *(MD II 116)*. Her will is on file *(Plymouth Colony Wills, Vol. III, part 2, pg. 12)*. Doty has had many descendants *(DG) MI)*, one of whom was Mrs. Russell Sage.

35—*Francis Eaton* came with his wife and son *(B 409)*. He was the twenty-third signer of the Mayflower Compact. He was a carpenter by occupation. He probably came from Bristol *(BK 52)* and has been called one of the London contingent *(HS I 21)*. He married, first, Sarah   ,who died at Plymouth, early in 1621, certainly after January 11. His second wife, whom he married at Plymouth, was believed to be "Mrs. Carver's maid." After her death, he married, third, at Plymouth, in 1624 or 1625, Christian Penn, a passenger on the "Ann" who survived her husband *(HX II 23)*. He died at Plymouth between November 4 and

18, 1633. Inventory of his estate has been published *(MD I 197-200)*. His widow married Francis Billington and died at Middleborough about 1684 *(MD II 116-117)*. He has had many descendants *(MI)*.

36—*Sarah (   ) Eaton*, first wife of Francis, came with her husband and son *(B 409)*. She died during the first general illness early in 1621 *(MD II 117) (B 413)*.

37—*Samuel ² Eaton* came as a baby with his parents *(B 409)*. He was born in 1620. He first lived with his father in Duxbury, but when he reached maturity, he moved to Middleboro. In 1636, with approval of his mother, he bound himself as an apprentice to John Cooke, Jr., for seven years *(PCR I 143)*. There is a record, "in the year next before 1652 the General Court admonished Samuel Eaton and Goodwife Hall, of Duxbury, for mixed dancing." *(HX II 23)*. He was something of a real estate speculator. He married, first, before March 20, 1647, Elizabeth   , who died between 1652 and 1661. He married, second, at Plymouth, January 20, 1661, Martha Billington, daughter of Francis and grand-daughter of Pilgrim John. Samuel died at Middleboro in 1684 before November 8. His inventory has been published *(MD II 172-173) (Plymouth Colony Wills and Invent., Vol. IV, part 1, pg. 83)*. His wife died after November 8, 1684 *(MD II 117)*. He has had many descendants.

38—*Ely,* whose first name is unknown was hired to stay a year. He did not sign the Mayflower Compact, probably because he did not intend to remain. When his time was out, he returned to England *(B 409)*. He was not known as Ellis in any source record. He left no known descendants.

39—*Thomas English* was a seaman who was hired to be master of the shallop *(B 409)*. He was the thirty-ninth signer of the Mayflower Compact. He may have been a resident of Leyden because a Thomas English appears there in the records *(BK 53)*. He took part in the third expedition which left the "Mayflower" on December 16, 1620, in the shallop to find a suitable place for a permanent settlement. He thereafter took part in the First Encounter with the Indians and later landed and helped select Plymouth as the place for the permanent settlement *(MR 43) (B 9)*. He died in the general sickness at Plymouth between January 11 and April 10, 1621 *(MD II 117)*. He left no known descendants.

40—*Moses Fletcher* came alone *(B 409)*. He was the twenty-seventh signer of the Mayflower Compact. He came from St. Peter's, Sandwich, County Kent, England. He had a son Moses born there on October 10, 1602. He was a smith by occupation and is supposed to have been living in Leyden when the Pilgrim group sailed. *(BK 54)*. His first wife was Maria Evans, who died before November, 1613. He married, second, at Leyden, Holland, December 21, 1613, Sarah (   ) Dingby, widow of William Dingby and died at Plymouth between January 11 and April 10, 1621 *(MD II 117) (R 211)*. He left no descendants.

41—*Edward Fuller* came with his wife and son *(B 408)*. He was the twenty-first signer of the Mayflower Compact. He was baptized September 4, 1575, son of Robert Fuller of Redenhall, Norfolk, England *(FE 23)*. There is no record of him at Leyden. He probably joined his brother Samuel at Southampton when the "Mayflower" sailed *(BK 55)*. He died at Plymouth between January 11 and April 10, 1621. His wife died early in 1621, after January 11 in the first general sickness *(MD II 117)*. They have had many descendants *(FE) (MI)*, including Chief Justice Melville Weston Fuller of the United States Supreme Court.

42—*Ann (   ) Fuller*, unmarried name unknown, came with her husband and son *(B 408)*. She died early in 1621 in the general sickness *(MD II 117) (HX II 19)*.

43—*Samuel ² Fuller*, son of Edward and Ann Fuller came with his parents *(B 408)*. He was born about 1612. He was made a freeman of the Colony in 1634. He went from Plymouth to Scituate on April 8, 1635, and joined the church there on November 7, 1636. On the day he arrived in Scituate he married Jane Lothrop, daughter of Rev. John. She was born at Edgerly, Kent, England, on September 29, 1614. They were in Barnstable by 1644, and he is the only "Mayflower" passenger who settled there. His wife died at Barnstable on October 31, 1683 *(HX II 19)*. He died at Barnstable on November 10, 1683 *(MD II 117)*. His will has been published *(MD II 237-241) (Plymouth Colony Wills and Invent., vol. IV, part 2, pgs. 138-139)*. He has had many descendants *(MI)*.

44—*Mr. Samuel Fuller* came leaving his wife and a child to come afterwards. He brought a servant William Butten. *(B 407)*. He was the eighth signer of the Mayflower Compact. He was the son of Robert Fuller and was baptized January 20, 1580, at Redenhall, County Norfolk, England *(FS 10)*. He was called a serge maker of London, but he later was also a doctor. He was Deacon of the Church in Leyden and at Plymouth *(HX I 23)*. He was married first to Alice or Elsie Glascock, who died before 1613. He married, second, at Leyden, Holland, on March 15, 1613 *(BK 56)*, Agnes, daughter of Alexander Carpenter *(MD VIII 129-130)* who died before 1617. He married, third, at Leyden, Holland, 27 May 1617, Bridget Lee *(MD VIII 129-130) (R 212)*. She was daughter of Joyce Lee and a sister of Samuel Lee. She came over in the "Anne." Samuel Fuller was an able letter writer *(B 70-71)*. In 1624, he interceded for The Rev. John Lyford and was referred to by Bradford as a "tender hearted" man *(B 189)*. In 1629, he was sent to Salem where many of the newly arrived colonists under John Endicott were very ill. On May 11, the latter wrote to Bradford expressing appreciation of Dr. Fuller's services *(B 260)*. He was an Assistant in 1632. He was the first physician to settle in New England. Bradford called him "a man godly, and forward to doe good, being missed after his death." *(B 302)*. He died at Plymouth between August 9 and September 26, 1633. His will *(MD I 24)* and inventory have been published *(MD II 8) (Plymouth Colony Wills and Invent., Vol.*

I, Fol. 22). His widow died after March 11, 1664 *(MD II 117)*. He has had many descendants, *(FS) (MI)*, including George A. Fuller, the construction engineer.

45—*Richard Gardiner* came alone *(B 409)*. He is described as a seaman employed by the company to remain *(BK 57)*. He has been identified as son of John and Lucy (Russell) Gardiner of Harwich, County Essex, and so related by marriage to Captain Christopher Jones *(BK 57)*. He was a man of some education because he and some other author are thought to have written the Nauset and Nemasket narratives which were sent on the "Fortune" by John Pierce, a friend of the Pilgrims, and later were delivered to George Morton *(B 12)*. He was the thirty-seventh signer of the Mayflower Compact. He was living late in 1624, but though he partook of the division of lands early in that year, he had no share in the division of cattle in 1627. No more is known of him except that he died in England or at sea between 1624 and 1651 *(MD II 117)*. He left no descendants.

46—*John Goodman* came alone *(B 409)*. He came from Leyden where he had married Sarah Hooper in 1619. He brought two dogs on the "Mayflower." He was the twenty-eighth signer of the Mayflower Compact. He had a lot assigned to him on Leyden Street in Plymouth in 1620 *(BK 58)*. On January 12, 1621, he had the adventures with Peter Brown in the woods already described in connection with the latter *(MR 73-74) (T 31)*. On January 19, 1621, not satisfied with his former experiences, he decided to ramble again in the woods with his spaniel. The dog was attacked by two wolves and fled to the legs of his master for safety. Goodman had no weapon except a stick. The wolves sat some time, snarling at him but at length let him escape *(MR 77-78) (T 32)*. He died at Plymouth before 1627 *(MD II 117)*. He left no descendants. He never changed his name to Dunham.

47—*William Holbeck* came as a servant of William White *(B 408)*. He did not sign the Mayflower Compact probably because he did not intend to stay. He is credited as one of the Leyden contingent *(BK 59)*. His family name is found in St. Andrew's parish in Norwich where the Rev. John Robinson was before he went to Leyden. He died without issue in the first winter *(BK 59)* early in 1621, after January 11 *(MD II 117)*.

48—*John Hooke* was described as a servant boy of Isaac Allerton *(B 407)*. He was too young to sign the Mayflower Compact. He is credited as one of the London contingent *(BK 60) (HS II 149)*. He died at Plymouth early in 1621 *(B 410-411)*, after January 11 *(MD II 117)*. He left no descendants.

49—*Mr. Stephen Hopkins* of London came with his second wife and his four children. Giles and Constance were from a previous marriage. Damaris and Oceanus were from the second marriage. He also brought two servants, Edward Doty and Edward Leister *(B 408)*. He was the fourteenth signer of the Mayflower Compact. He is probably the person who had a son Stephen baptized December 22, 1609. The name of his first wife is alleged to be Constance Dudley in "The Compendium of American Genealogy," but I do not know the basis for the statement. His second marriage was to Elizabeth Fisher, February 19, 1617/18 at St. Mary Matfellon (White Chapel), London. *(BK 61 (HX 24)*.

Stephen Hopkins was one of the passengers on the "Sea Venture" of 300 tons, which was one of a fleet of seven ships and two pinnaces which started a voyage to Virginia on July 23, 1609.* On the vessel were the "sturdy soldier" Sir Thomas Gates, Deputy Governor of the Virginia Colony, and "the old sea rover" Sir George Summers, Admiral of the Seas. The Captain was the famous Christopher Newport who had made many trips, including the first, between England and Virginia. When about seven or eight days sail from their destination, a terrible storm arose which lasted for several days. The "Sea Venture" became a wreck and on July 28, 1609, was driven ashore on the Island of Bermuda

*See page 196.

where the passengers and crew to the number of 150 men, women and children alighted by means of their small boats. There were no inhabitants there probably because of Spanish slave hunters. Fortunately there were a great number of birds on the island which were tame and easily caught. There were also thousands of wild hogs on the island which were probably descendants of those left on the island by Oviedo in the year 1515. There were also many turtles.

Attempts were made to build vessels so that the voyage might be continued. On September 1st, a conspiracy was discovered which was suppressed. The connection of Stephen Hopkins with a later conspiracy is described as follows in "Shipwrecks and Disasters at Sea," pages 9 and 10, published in London by H. G. Bohn in 1856:

"Yet this could not be a warning to others, who began more insidiously to shake the foundations of our peace and tranquility. Stephen Hopkins, a fellow of considerable knowledge in the Scriptures, who had been chosen by our minister as clerk, to read the psalms and chapters on Sundays, to the people assembled, leagued with Samuel Sharp and Humphrey Reed, on the 24th of January, alleging, by arguments both civil and divine, that it was no breach of honesty, conscience, nor religion, to decline the authority of the governor. He urged that, in point of conscience, even the meanest must be sensible how much each was bound to provide for himself and his whole family, whence there were two evident reasons for remaining here: first, by God's providence, abundance of food; secondly, the prospect that, in a reasonable time, they might grow weary of it, and then build a small bark with the help of Nicholas Bennet, who, although now absent assisting Sir George Summers, they insinuated, was of the conspiracy. By such means they might get free of this country when they pleased; but, if they went to Virginia, they should assuredly want provisions, and might well apprehend that they would be detained there by the authority of the commander, and thenceforth ever be bound to serve the purposes of the adventurers.

"Sharp and Reed, however, disclosed the conspiracy, on which the governor ordered Hopkins to be seized and brought out in irons before the whole people; where, after hearing his accusation, he was allowed to plead an exculpation to every particular fact laid to his charge. It was proved, nevertheless, that he was the ringleader and promoter of the mutiny; and the general opinion was that his life should atone for the offence; therefore the governor, by a court martial, sentenced him to that punishment which rebellion deserves. But he behaved with such penitence, made so much lamentation, and so pathetically deplored the ruin of his wife and children, which would be the consequence of his trespass, that compassion was excited in all the higher orders of our company. Thus they repaired to the Governor, and besought him to pardon the culprit, which, after much entreaty, he consented to do."

It was not until May 21, 1610, that was[*]left of the passengers of the "Sea Venture" reached Virginia in a small boat which they had built in Bermuda. It is related that the voyagers found the Virginia Colony in a distressed condition. The buildings were going to waste. The scarcity of provisions increased daily. In a short time hardly sixty of six hundred settlers survived and these were starving. Gates, Somers and Newport determined to abandon the settlement which would have been accomplished except for the arrival of Lord Delaware with supplies from England. The wreck of the "Sea Venture" is said by the historian John Fiske to have suggested to Shakespeare many hints for the "Tempest," which was written within the next two years and performed before the King in 1611. It seems clear that Shakespeare made use of Strachey's narrative of the wreck of the "Sea Venture" which was published in 1610.

Hopkins could not have met Captain John Smith in

*See page 196.

Virginia because it was in October, 1609, that Smith, after being wounded by an explosion of gun powder, returned to England for surgical treatment. When Smith's health had been restored, he formed a partnership with certain London merchants with the idea of obtaining some profits for the Plymouth Company from its American grant. This led to his expedition to the New England Coast in 1614 and his unsuccessful attempt to send over two other vessels later. Hopkins returned to England on an unknown date, and he must have been in a position where he could meet Smith had he desired to do so. One reason why the historians believed that the Stephen Hopkins of the "Sea Venture" and the Stephen Hopkins of the "Mayflower" are the same persons is because of the knowledge of America which Hopkins had. When the Pilgrims were on their first exploring party and Bradford had been caught in an Indian trap made by a noose attached to a bent tree, Hopkins explained that it was an Indian trap for deer (B 8-9). He was sent with Standish to try to interview strange Indians (MR 81). When Samoset came to Plymouth, he stayed overnight in the house of Hopkins, probably because Hopkins knew more about Indians than the others (MR 85). It was Hopkins who went in early July, 1621, with Winslow to confirm the treaty with Massasoit and to strengthen amicable relations between the settlers and the Indians (M 48) (MR 98-111) (B 10) (B 117). When a messenger came from Cononicus bringing the snake skin full of arrows, Hopkins was able to learn from the Indian what it meant. It seems probable that Hopkins was selected by Weston to accompany the Pilgrims because of his previous experiences in Virginia. (BK 61-64) (HS I 117).

Hopkins was a member of the first expedition which proceeded by land on November 25, 1620 (MR 13-14), and also the third expedition which started in the shallop on December 16, 1620, and which engaged in the first encounter on December 18, 1620, and eventually landed at and selected Plymouth as a settlement *(MR 43)*. He was an Assistant from 1633 to 1636. He was a volunteer in the Pequot War in 1637. His second wife died at Plymouth between 1640 and 1644 *(MD II 117) (BK 61)*. He was a member of the Council of War for the Colony, 1642 to 1644. He was mentioned several times in court orders *(HS I 120-121)*. He died at Plymouth between June 16 and July 27, 1644. His daughters are described *(MD IV 114) (MD V 47)*. His will and inventory have been published *(MD II 12) (Plymouth Colony Wills and Invent., vol. I, folios 61, 62 and 63)*. He had many descendants *(AM 19/536), (HB), (MI)*, including John Howard Payne, author of "Home Sweet Home", Major General Amiel Weeks Whipple, the explorer of the Southwest and Colonel Charles W. Whiffle.

50—*Elizabeth (Fisher) Hopkins* came with her husband, two children and two step-children *(B 408)*. She died at Plymouth between 1640 and 1644 *(MD II 117) (BK 61)*.

51—*Gyles ² Hopkins* was born about 1607. He was a child of Stephen Hopkins by a former marriage and came with his father and step-mother, also with his sister Constance and his half-sister Damaris and half-brother Oceanus born on the "Mayflower" *(B 408)*. He was a volunteer in the Pequot War in 1637. He married October 19, 1639, Katherine Wheldon and removed to Yarmouth. She died after March 15, 1689. He died before April 26, 1690 *(MD II 117)*. His will has been published *(HS I 138-139) (Probate Records of Barnstable County, vol. I, pg. 32)*. He left many descendants. (MI).

52—*Constance ² Hopkins,* child of Stephen Hopkins by a former marriage came in the family of her father and step-mother *(B 408)*. She was born about 1605 *(HS I 126)*. She married at Plymouth between 1623 and June 1, 1627, probably about 1626, Nicholas Snow of Hexton, Middlesex, England. In 1644, many families determined to leave Plymouth and to settle in Eastham. Nicholas Snow was one of this number. He was town clerk in Eastham from 1646 to 1662. He died at Eastham, November 25, 1676. His will has been published *(HS I 126-128). (Plymouth Colony Wills and Invent., vol. III, Part II, pages 71-77).* She died there in October, 1677 *(MD II 118), (AM 19/536).* They have many descendants *(MI).* Bradford calls her "Constanta."

53—*Damaris ² Hopkins* was born probably before 1619 *(MD V 50-51).* She came with her parents, a sister, a half-sister and a half-brother *(B 408).* She died young, unmarried. A second daughter of the same name, not a "Mayflower" passenger, married Jacob Cooke after June 20, 1646, possibly early in 1647 *(MD V 51-52).*

54—*Oceanus ² Hopkins,* son of Stephen and Elizabeth Hopkins, was born on the "Mayflower" between September 16, and November 21, 1620. He died before June 1, 1627 *(MD II 118).*

55—*John Howland,* son of Henry Howland of Fen Stanton, Huntingdonshire, England, came as a servant of John Carver *(B 407).* He was the thirteenth signer of the Mayflower Compact. He is credited to London. John Howland was identified because the will of Humphrey Howland, citizen and draper of St. Swithin's, London, proved July 10, 1646, mentions his four brothers, George, Arthur, John and Henry, the last three in New England *(BK 65).*

Leon C. Hills of Washington, D.C., well-known genealogist, has gathered much material concerning the Howland family, especially from the Parish Registers of Holy Trinity, in Cambridgeshire, Ely, and of Fen Stanton also the Visitations of London and Cambridgeshire. Henry Howland married first Alice Aires on April 26, 1600, at St. Mary's, Ely. It is probably her initials that are on the pewter mentioned in Humphrey's will. She was probably the mother of John. Henry married, second, Margaret, last name unknown, who was buried in Fen Stanton on July 31, 1629. Henry Howland was buried in Fen Stanton on May 17, 1635 *(AG 14-215).* A tentative list of Henry's children is as follows:

1—Humphrey, a London citizen and draper, born about 1600, died in England in 1646, married Annie, last name unknown. He was apprenticed to James Smith, November 19, 1613, and was made free December 1, 1620.

2—John, baptized January 16, 1602/3 in Holy Trinity, Ely. He became the Pilgrim.

3—Henry, baptized November 25, 1604, married Mary Newland and died in Duxbury on January 17, 1671. She died in Duxbury on June 16, 1674.

4—Simon, baptized August 19, 1604/5 in Fen Stanton. He married Ann Ulster in 1632 and died in England in 1634, leaving children. Both he and Henry were apprenticed for a time to Humphrey.

5—Margaret, married on April 26, 1623, to Richard Phillips; had ten children born between 1623 and 1654 in Fen Stanton and died in England.

6—George, died in 1643 in England. He was a London Merchant.

7—Arthur, married Margaret Reed, widow, and died in 1675 in Marshfield. His widow died in 1683.

8—William, baptized February   , 1610/11 in Holy Trinity, Ely. He died before 1646 in England.

The foregoing would make John Howland just over seventy at the time of his death if he was baptized shortly after birth. This conflicts with the statement of Morton that John Howland "lived until he attained above eighty years in the world." It also conflicts with the Plymouth Church Records which state that he died in his eightieth year. The records seem to identify John's family, and the statements concerning his age at death would seem to be a mistake. Bradford describes this incident on the "Mayflower;" "In sundrie of these stormes the winds were so feirce; and the seas so high, as they could not beare a knote of saile, but were forced to hull, (drift), for diverce days togither. And in one of them, as they thus lay at hull, in a mighty storme, a lustie yonge man (called John Howland) coming upon some occasion above the gratings, was with a seele of the shipe (meaning toss in a rough sea) throwne into (the) sea; but it pleased God that he caught hould of the top-saile halliards, which hunge over board ,and rane out at length; yet he held his hould (though he was sundrie fadomes under water) till he was hald up by the same rope to the brime of the water, and then with a boat hooke and other means got into the shipe againe, and his life saved; and though he was some thing ill with it, yet he lived many years after, and became a profitable member both in church and commone wealth" *(B 94)*. The names of all of those who participated in the first two expeditions on shore from the "Mayflower" have not been preserved. He was a member of the third expedition on the shallop which left the "Mayflower" on December 16, 1620, and which participated in the first encounter with the Indians on December 18, 1620, at what was later Eastham and which landed on the Rock at Plymouth and selected that spot as the permanent settlement *(MR 43)*. He married at Plymouth before 1624, Elizabeth, daughter of John and Elizabeth Tilley, who was born about 1607. In the early spring of 1624, four acres of land were assigned to John Howland who had succeeded to be the head of John Carver's family group. In 1626, he was one of the men who assumed the debt of the Colony. John Howland was an Assistant from 1633 to 1635 and was elected a Deputy to the General Court in 1641. In April, 1634, when he was in command of the Kennebec trading post, a Mr. John Hocking killed one of his men and was in turn killed by another of Howland's men. One of Hocking's kinsmen in Boston pursued the matter so this made much trouble between Plymouth and Massachusetts Colonies, *(N. E. IX, 80) (Maine Coll. 3, 1, 322)* but the matter quickly died out when the true facts were known. *(MD II 10-11)*. In the preparations for the Pequot War, he was one of those appointed to arrange for Plymouth's share. Meadow land was granted to him in 1636 at Island Creek, Duxbury. Numerous other grants were given to him. Because of his liberality to the Quakers, he was dropped as Deputy to the General Court in 1659 and 1660 but was reelected in 1661 and served until 1670. He lived during his latter years in his home at Rocky Nook where he died March 5, 1673 *(MD II 70) (Plymouth Colonies Wills and Invent., Vol. III, part I, pgs. 49-54)*. He was buried on Burial Hill. Many years later a stone was placed where he was thought to have been buried. Morton said of him, "Hee was a godly man and an ancient professor in the wayes of Christ:"

"He was one of the first comers to this land, and proved a useful instrument of good in his place and was the last man that was left of those that came over in the shipp called the Mayflower that lived in Plymouth:" His widow died at Swansea, 31 December 1687 *(MD II 118)(MD III 54)*. John Howland's will and inventory are published *(MD II 70)*. They have had many descendants, of whom I shall mention only a few. Among them are Franklin Delano Roosevelt, President of the United States; Lt.-Colonel John Gorham, who had been in command of the expedition against the French in 1703-1704; Nathaniel Gorham, member of the Convention which framed the U. S. Constitution; Joseph Smith, founder of the Mormon Church; Phillips Brooks, Episcopal Bishop of Massachusetts; Parker H. Fillmore, author; Major General Adolphus Washington Greely, the Arctic explorer; William T. Davis, the historian; Henry Cabot Lodge, U. S. Senator; Henry Billings Brown, Associate Justice of the U. S. Supreme Court; Foster Stearns, Congressman from New Hampshire; Abbot Augustus Low, the legislator; Seth Low; Allen Wardwell, the lawyer; McClure Meredith Howland, President of the Pilgrim John Howland Society; and the Honorable Henry E. Howland, jurist and First Governor General of the Society of Mayflower Descendants. Among the distinguished women descended from him are Lillian Russell and Maude Adams, actresses; also Jane Austen, the writer of Plymouth stories. Winston Churchill, British Prime Minister is descended from John's brother Henry Howland.

56—*John Langmore* came as a servant of Christopher Martin *(B 408)*. He was one of the Leyden contingent *(BK 66)*. He did not sign the Mayflower Compact. He was possibly originally a resident of Essex. He died at Plymouth early in 1621 and after January 11, in the general sickness of the first winter without known issue *(BK 66) (MD II 118)*.

57—*William Latham,* a boy, came in the family of John Carver *(B 407)*. He was too young to sign the Mayflower Compact. He was taxed in Plymouth in 1632. He later resided in Duxbury. He returned to England after 1641 and according to Bradford, emigrated to the Bahamas, West Indies, where he died from starvation without known issue *(BK 67)* between November 7, 1645 and March 6, 1651 *(MD II 118) (HS II 215)*.

58—*Edward Leister* came as a servant of Stephen Hopkins *(B 408)*. He was the forty-first and last signer of the Mayflower Compact. He came from London. On June 18, 1621, he fought a duel with Edward Doty, and as a result both men had their heads and feet tied together but were released by the governor after one hour of such punishment *(T 38)*. After he was at liberty to do so, he moved to Virginia *(B 414)*. He may have been a member of a family living in the parish of St. Mary, Kensington, a suburb of London *(BK 68)*. He died in Virginia before March 6, 1651 *(MD II 118)*. Descent has been claimed from him, but none has been approved by the Society of Mayflower Descendants.

59—*Edmond Margeson* came alone *(B 409)*. He was the thirty-second signer of the Mayflower Compact. It has been claimed that this name may be an error for Edmund Masterson who was father of Deacon Richard Masterson of Leyden who came to Plymouth on another ship also named the "Mayflower" which arrived in Salem on May 15, 1629. *(HS II 218) (BK 69)*. The Society of Mayflower Descendants has not accepted Edmond as the father of Richard. Whether Edmond has descendants depends on this relationship because Richard has many. He died at Plymouth between January 11 and April 10, 1621, in the first general sickness *(MD II 118)*.

60—*Mr. Christopher Martin* came with his wife and two servants, his stepson, Solomon Prower, and John Langmore *(B 408)*. He came from Essex. He married the Widow Marie Prower on February 26, 1606/7, at Great Burstead in Essex. On March 3, 1619/20, he was prosecuted in the Archdeaconal Court for "suffering his son (Solomon Prower) to answer him (i.e. the Archdeacon) that his father gave him his name" *(NE 21-77) (BK 70)*. He may be found as a taxpayer early in 1620 in the Parish of St. Bartholomew the Great in London *(BK 78)*. Martin became interested in the Virginia company of Merchant Adventurers. One historian thinks he might have been one of those who went to Jamestown, Virginia, in 1609 *(HS II 217)*. He is mentioned by Bradford as follows: "Besids these things, ther fell out a difference amongs those 3 that received the moneys and made the provisions in England; for besids these tow formerly mentioned sent from Leyden for this end, viz. Mr. Carver and Robert Cushman, there was one chosen in England to be joyned with them, to make the provisions for the vioage; his name was Mr. Martin, he came from Billirike in Essexe, from which parts came sundrie others to goe with them, as also from London and other places; and therefore it was thought meete and conveniente by them in Holand that these strangers that were to goe with them, should apointe one thus to be joyned with them, not so much for any great need of their help, as to avoyd all susspition, or jelosie of any partiallitie" *(B 76)*. In a letter dated June 10, 1620, from Robert Cushman to John Carver appears the following: "Yea, ther was a schisme amongst us 3 at the first. You wrote to Mr. Martin, to prevente the making of the provissions in Kente, which he did, and sett

donne his resolution how much he would have of everything, without respecte to any counsell or exception. Surely
he that is in a societie and yet regards not counsell, may
better be a king than a consorte" *(B 77)*. He later amended
the conditions agreed to by the Pilgrims to their great dis-
pleasure *(B 81-82)*. In a letter from Robert Cushman dated
August 17, 1620, to Edward Southworth is the following:
"And Mr. Martine, he said he never received no money on
those conditions, he was not beholden to the merchants for
a fine, they were bloudsuckers, and I know not what. Simple
man, he indeed never made any conditions with the merchants, nor ever spake wtih them. But did all that money
flie to Hampton, or was it his owne? Who will goe and lay
out money so rashly and lavishly as he did, and never know
how he comes by it or on what conditions? 2 ly. I tould him
of the alteration longe agoe, and he was contente; but now
he dominires, and said I had betrayed them into the hands
of slaves; he is not beholden to them, he can set out 2. ships
him selfe to a viage. When, good man? He hath but 50 li.
in, and if he should give up his accounts he would not have
a penie left him, as I am persuaded" *(B 91)*. This last statement was afterwards found to be true. He acted as Governor
of the "Mayflower," representing the Virginia Company of
London. He was the ninth signer of the Mayflower Compact. He died during the great sickness at Plymouth on
January 18, 1621. His wife died early in 1621, after January
11 *(MD II 118)*. They left no descendants.

61—*Marie (   ) (Prower) Martin* came over with her
husband, Christopher Martin and her son by a former marriage Solomon Prower *(MD II 118) (B 408) (BK 70)*. She
died during the first general sickness. Her maiden name is
unknown.

62—*Desire Minter* came with the family of John Carver
(B 407) and some time after he had died returned to Eng-
land and died there unmarried as far as is known. A William
Minter of Norwich, England, emigrated to Leyden, was

granted citizenship there in 1613 and died before 1618, leaving a widow, Sarah, who was the daughter of Thomas and Alice Willett of Norwich. These last were parents of Thomas Willett who came to Plymouth in 1629 and with William Paddy became one of the outstanding merchants. When the English captured New Amsterdam, he became the first English Mayor of New York City. It is possible that Desire was connected with this Minter family *(BK 71)*.

63—*Jasper More,* son of Samuel and Kathrine More, was "a child that was put to" John Carver *(B 407)* apparently at the request of Merchant Adventurer Thomas Weston for the purpose of subsistence. He was baptized on August 8, 1613, in the parish of Shipton, County Salop, England *(BK 72)*. He came from an ancient family previously described herein *(NY 36-214)*. He was too young to sign the Mayflower Compact. He died at Cape Cod Harbor on December 16, 1620 *(MD II 118)*.

64—*Ellen More,* daughter of Samuel and Kathrine More of Shipton, Shropshire, England, was a little girl who "was put to" Edward Winslow, arrangements apparently being made by Thomas Weston. She was a sister of Jasper, Richard and the other More brother, *(B 407)*, who came over on the "Mayflower." She was baptized in Shipton, County Salop on May 24, 1612. She died at Plymouth early in 1621, after January 11 *(MD II 118)*.

65—*Richard More,* son of Samuel and Katherine More, was a boy "put to" William Brewster *(B 407)*. More was baptized in the parish of Shipton, County Salop, on November 3, 1614. *(MD V 256) (NY 36-213)*. He made an affidavit on September 27, 1684, in which he says he was "aged seaventy yeares or thereabouts" and tells that he was living in the house of Mr. Thomas Weston, ironmonger, in London, in 1620" and was thence transported to New Plymouth in New England *(NE 50-203) (MD III 194-195)*. This Weston was a leader among the Merchant Adventurers who financed the voyage of the "Mayflower" *(BK 72)*. This affidavit, in addition to the published records of the More family, shows the untruthfulness of statements made to the effect that he and his brothers and sister were waifs picked up in London. Mr. Weston must have known the parents of the More children and obviously saw that they were assigned to families of several of the most outstanding of the Pilgrims. More was still in the Brewster family at the division of cattle in 1627 *(MD III 194)*. Richard More married October 30, 1636, Christian Hunt *(PCR I 45)*, born about 1616, and on November 11, 1637, he sold his house and adjoining land at Duxbury *(MD I 150) (MD II 118)*. He had other lands at Swansen,* Taunton and other places. His wife Christian died at Salem, Massachusetts, on March 28, 1677. He married, second, Jane Hollingsworth, born about 1631 and who died at Salem, on October 18, 1686 *(MD III 198)*. He was a mariner and was known as Captain. He died at Salem between March 29, 1694 and April 30, 1696, and his gravestone still stands there in the old Charter Street Cemetery. *(MD III 193) (MD IV 128)*. He had descendants.

66—   *More*, first name is unknown. He was son of Samuel and Katherine More and was "put to" William Brewster *(B 407)*, apparently by arrangement of Merchant Adventurer Weston. His baptism is not found in the registers of the parish of Shipton, County Salop, England, where those of his sister and brothers have been found. He die at Plymouth in the general sickness early in 1621, after January 11 *(MD II 118)*.

67—*Mr. William Mullins* came with his wife and two children and a servant Robert Carter *(B 408)*. He was the tenth signer of the Mayflower Compact. He seems to have been residing at Stoke, near Guildford, County Surrey. This was about ten miles from Dorking. He was living in the latter place in 1612 because he is recorded as having a holding there that year which he sold in May, 1619, before he left England. He was concerned in the religious troubles of the times. In the records of the Privy Council for April

*See page 196.

29, 1616, is recorded a warrant issued to arrest him and to bring him before the Lords of Council. On May 1, he appeared before the Council and was continued in its custody "untill by their Honour's order hee be dismissed." He owned nine shares in the Adventurers' Company and is listed among the London contingent *(HX I 25)*. He married Alice   , who survived him. He died during the first great sickness at Plymouth on March 3, 1621 *(MD II 118) (MD I 88)*. His will was prepared on the "Mayflower" and was witnessed by Governor Carver, by Dr. Giles Heale, Surgeon of the "Mayflower," and by Captain Christopher Jones, Commander of the "Mayflower" *(BK 74) (MD I 230-232) (NE, XLII, 62)*. When he died, he left an estate largely composed of boots and shoes. His widow died shortly after him at Plymouth after April 2 in 1621 *(MD II 118)*.

He left behind in England a son and daughter apparently by a first marriage. William Mullins, Jr., the eldest· son, was left in England and was married there in 1617. Three of the latter's children were baptized in Dorking and the son himself came to New England in 1636. The elder daughter Sarah married a Blunden and administered her father's estate. *(BK 73-74)*. William Mullins had many descendants *(MI)*, some of whom are mentioned under John Alden, his son-in-law. Bradford calls him "Mullines also Molines," which may be the Walloon form.

68—*Alice (   ) Mullins* was the second wife of her husband and was the mother of Priscilla and Joseph Mullins. Her maiden name is unknown. She died shortly after her husband *(MD II 118)*.

69—*Joseph ² Mullins* was issue of William Mullins by his second wife Alice. He died at Plymouth after April 2, early in 1621 *(MD II 118)*.

70—*Priscilla Mullins* was issue of William by his second wife Alice *(BK 74)*. She was born about 1602. She married John Alden and has received much publicity because she was made the heroine of "The Courtship of Myles Standish" by Henry Wadsworth Longfellow. The poem is founded on what had been handed down by tradition in Plymouth. She had many descendants *(MI)*. There is no evidence of the date of her death except she was present with her husband at Josiah Winslow's funeral in 1680. She must have died before her husband, for his 1686 will does not mention her *(CE 79)*.

71—*Degory Priest* came alone *(B 409)*. He was the twenty-ninth signer of the Mayflower Compact. He was born about 1579 *(MD II 118)* and is credited as one of the Leyden contingent. In the Leyden records he is called a hatter from London. He married at Leyden, Holland, on November 4, 1611, Sarah (Allerton) Vincent, sister of Isaac Allerton and widow of John Vincent of London. *(R 213) (MD VII 129-130) (DN 630)*. He was admitted a burgess in 1615. He died at Plymouth on January 11, 1621, in the "general sickness" aged about forty-two years *(MD I 87) (MD II 118)*. He left two daughters, Mary and Sarah, who came on the "Anne" with their mother *(BK 75)*. His widow married Cuthbert Cuthbertson, a Dutchman, who also was of the Leyden Company. Winslow calls him Godbert Godbertson *(HX II 24)*. She died at Plymouth before November 3, 1633 *(MD II 118)*. He has had many descendants *(MI)*, among them the philanthropist John Divine Jones, developer of marine insurance in the United States.

72—*Solomon Prower* came from Billerica, Essex, with his mother and stepfather Christopher Martin. He is described as a servant even though employed by his stepfather and mother *(B 408)*. He was possibly too young to sign the Mayflower Compact. On March 3, 1619/20, he was brought before the Archdeaconal Court at Chelmsford, Essex, for refusing to answer properly Archdeacon Pease's question "Who gave you your name in baptism?" His answer was that he did not know because his father was dead and he did not know his God-father's name. He was eventually discharged *(BK 76)*. He died at Plymouth in the first general sickness on January 3, 1621. *(MD II 118)*. He left no descendants.

73—*John Rigdale* came with his wife *(B 408)*. He was the twentieth signer of the Mayflower Compact. He was undoubtedly from London *(BK 77)*. He married Alice   , who died at Plymouth in the first general sickness, early in 1621, after January 11. He died at Plymouth, between January 11 and April 10, 1621 *(MD II 119)*. He left no descendants.

74—*Alice (   ) Rigdale* came with her husband *(B 408)* and died during the first winter. *(MD II 119)*. Her maiden name is unkown.

75—*Thomas Rogers* was perhaps born about 1587 *(HS I 131)* and came with his son Joseph. Other children came afterwards *(B 408)*. He was a "camlet" merchant. In London, he was a taxpayer in the parish of St. Bartholomew the Great *(BK 78)*. He was a member of the Congregation in Leyden on or before June 25, 1618, though he may have been in Leyden much earlier than that date. He acquired citizenship that year. Before sailing on the "Mayflower," he sold on April 1, 1620, a house on Barbara Lane, Leyden *(HS I 132)*. He was the eighteenth signer of the Mayflower Compact. Bradford says of him, "Thomas Rogers dyed in the first sicknes, but his sone Joseph is still living, and is maried, and hath 6 children. The rest of Thomas Rogers (children) came over, and are maried, and have many children" *(B 412)*. He died at Plymouth between January 11 and April 10, 1621. Nothing is known of his wife *(MD II 119)*. He has had many descendants *(MI)*.

76—*Joseph ² Rogers* came with his father *(B 408)*. He was too young to sign the Mayflower Compact. He married before 1633, but nothing is known of his wife except her name was Hannah *(MD II 119)*. In 1635, the court records state that "Joseph Rogers was allowed a constant ferry over the Jones River, neer his dwelling house, and to take a

149

penny for the transportation of each person, he, the said Joseph, maintayning a sufficient ferry at that price." He was constable in 1640. He and his brother John were on the list of men in Duxbury able to bear arms in August, 1643. He was later commissioned lieutenant. In 1648, leave was granted to him as Lieut. Joseph Rogers to have land purchased of Indians. Meanwhile he moved from Duxbury to Sandwich because on February 24, 1652, he was appointed "one of the jurors to lay out the most convenient way from Sandwich to Plymouth." On May 22, 1655, he was among the legal voters of Eastham. In 1658, he was a member of the Council of War for the Colony. He died at Eastham on November 9, 1678. The will has been published *(MD II 67)* (Plymouth Colony Wills, Vol. III, part 2, pgs. 103-105). His wife was living at Eastham on January 12, 1678 *(MD II 119)*. He has had many descendants *(MI)*.

77—*Henry Samson* came in the family of Edward and Mrs. Tilley whose cousin he was *(B 408)*. He was one of the London contingent *(BK 79)*. He was too young to sign the Mayflower Compact. He was a volunteer in the Pequot War in 1637. *(PCR I 60-61)*. He married at Plymouth on February 16, 1636, Ann Plummer, *(MD II 119) (PCR I 36)*, who was living January 3, 1669 *(MD IV 128)* and who died between that date and 1685. He died at Duxbury, January 3, 1685 *(MD II 119)*. His will and inventory have been published *(MD II 142)* (Plymouth County Wills and Invent., Vol. IV, part 2, pgs. 94-95). He had many descendants *(MI)* *(SH)*.

78—*George Soule* came as a servant of Edward Winslow *(B 407)*. He was the thirty-fifth signer of the Mayflower Compact. He was born about 1600 and is credited to the London contingent. He was the son of John Soule of Eckington. Robert Soule of the family was a London Salter. Droitwich, where Edward Winslow was born, was a salt mining place and connected with the Salters Company of London *(BK 80)*. This last may have brought George

Soule and Edward Winslow together. His *wife, Mary Bucket, came on the "Anne," and George Soule married her before 1627 *(BK 81)*. He was a volunteer for the Pequot War in 1637. He was Deputy to the General Court from Duxbury, 1645 to 1654. His wife died at Duxbury in December, 1676 *(MD II 81, 119)*. He died at Duxbury shortly before February, 1680, probably January *(MD II 81)* (Plymouth County Wills and Invent., Vol. IV, part 1, pg. 50). His autograph has been preserved, and it is "Soule." *(MD IV 98)*. He had many descendants *(MI) (SR)*.

79—*Captain Myles Standish* came with his wife Rose *(B 408)*. He was born in Lancashire *(B 98 note)* about 1584 *(HX 17)*, and was in military service in Holland during her war with Spain. During the twelve years' truce he found the Pilgrims in Leyden, and the result was that he came in the "Mayflower" with his wife Rose, who died at Plymouth on February 8, 1621. He was the sixth signer of the Mayflower Compact. He married, second, at Plymouth between July 1623, and April 3, 1624, Barbara, who may have come on the "Anne" or "Little James" in 1623. He was a leader in the explorations resulting in the selection of Plymouth as a permanent home *(MR 13-14, 43)*. He was one of the two who distinguished themselves in nursing the sick during the terrible first winter *(B 108)*. In 1623, he went to the rescue of Weston's men *(B 143-144)*. In 1625, he went to England to seek aid from the Council of New England on behalf of the Colony *(B 207)*. In 1628, he took as prisoner the rascally Thomas Morton, who was sent back to England *(B 242)*. He later received a grant of land in Duxbury which he occupied as early as 1630 *(B 363)*. The statement has been made that he was a Roman Catholic probably because some branches of his family were of that religion. Hubbard in his "General History of New England," page 63, describes him as a person who at that time was not of their church. The following entry in the Plymouth Colony records shows that he was a Protestant if

151

not a full member of the Plymouth Church when the record was made: "Anno 1632 Aprell 2—the names of those which promise to remove their families to live in the town in the winter time that they may the better repaire to the worship of God—John Alden, Capt. Standish, Jonathan Brewster, Thomas Prence." The list of his books *(MD III 155)* shows that he had a number of Protestant books *(NE 68-342)*. He was the captain and military leader of Plymouth Colony from 1621 and assistant from 1631 to 1650. For six years he was treasurer of the Colony. In 1649, he was made Commander-in-Chief for all the Colony. He died at Duxbury, October 13, 1656 *(MD III 153)*. (Plymouth County Wills and Invent., Vol. II, part 1, pgs. 37-40). His widow died after October 16, 1659 *(MD II 119)*. His will described lands of which he had been deprived *(MD III 153)*. He has had many distinguished descendants *(MI) (SW)* including Burnham Standish Colburn and Mrs. Alton Brooks Parker.

80—*Rose (   ) Standish* came with her husband *(B 408)*. The maiden name of this first wife of Myles is unknown.

81—*Elias Story* came as a servant of Edward Winslow *(B 407)*. He did not sign the Mayflower Compact. He came from London *(BK 84)*. He died at Plymouth in the first general sickness after January 11, early in 1621 *(MD II 119)*. He left no known descendants.

82—*Edward Thomson* came as a servant of William White *(B 408)*. He did not sign the Mayflower Compact. He died on the "Mayflower" at Cape Cod Harbor on December 14, 1620 *(MD II 119)*. His was the first death after their arrival at Cape Cod. He left no issue *(BK 85)*.

83—*Edward Tilley* is not the Edward Tilley, son of Lawrence and Bridget Tilley, baptized October 29, 1574, at Shipton, County Salop, England, *(NY 35-213, 291)*, because that Edward had a wife named Lucia who died January 4, 1629 *(BK 86)*. Also the John Tilley, brother of that Edward, is obviously not our John. Edward may be related to the

Shipton family. He came with his wife and two children who were their cousins, Henry Samson and Humility Cooper *(B 408)*. He was the fifteenth signer of the Mayflower Compact and came from London *(BK 86)*. He was added as counsel to the first expedition which left the "Mayflower" on November 21, 1620 *(MR 13-14) (B 8)*. The names of the persons who took part in the second expedition are unknown. He was a member of the third expedition which left the "Mayflower" in the shallop on December 16, 1620, and which had the First Encounter with the Indians on December 18, 1620, and which thereafter made the historic landing on the rock at Plymouth *(MR 43) (B 9)*. His wife Ann died at Plymouth after January 11, early in 1621. He died at Plymouth between January 11, and April 10, 1621 *(MD II 119)*. They are not known to have left any descendants. Bradford calls him "Tillie," but "Tilley" is the spelling in Morton. "Tilly" is wrong.

84—*Ann (   ) Tilley* came with her husband and their two cousins, Humility Cooper and Henry Samson *(B 408)*. Her maiden name is unknown as is the date of her marriage.

85—*John Tilley* came with his wife and Elizabeth their daughter *(B 408)*. He was the sixteenth signer of the Mayflower Compact. He is not the John Tilley, son of Lawrence and Bridget Tilley of Shipton, County Salop, England, who was baptized February 24, 1571 *(NY 35-213, 291)* because the latter John was living in Shipton in 1631, long after our John was dead *(BK 87)*. Our John may be John Tilley, yeoman, who was living in Wooton, Bedfordshire, in 1613, aged forty years, and hence born in 1573. John Tilley was apparently the one who was married to Elizabeth Comyngs on February 2, 1605, in the parish of St. Andrew Undershaft *(BK 87)*. There is no evidence that he was ever in Leyden. He was a member of the third expedition *(M 31)* which left the "Mayflower" in the shallop on December 16, 1620, and which had the First Encounter with the Indians on December 18, 1620 *(M 32-33)*, and which thereafter made the historic landing on the rock at Plymouth *(MR 43)*, *(B 9)*. His wife died at Plymouth in the first general sickness after January 11, early in 1621. He died at Plymouth between January 11 and April 10, 1621 *(MD II 119)*. They have many descendants *(MI)* some of whom are mentioned under the name of his son-in-law John Howland.

In spite of all statements to the contrary, Jan Tellji of Leyden was not the English John Tilley of the "Mayflower."

The record of the betrothal at Leyden on 13 February, 1615, of "Jan Tellji" and "Prijntgen Van der Velde" is found in the "Kerkelicke Huwelycke Proclamatie Boeck," folio 48 verso, with other betrothals of the same date. The marriage took place in 3 March, 1615.

The betrothal records read as follows:

"(The Dutch Record)

"Jan Telliji saeywercker Jongman van Leyden verge-selschapt met Paulus Telly zyn vader

met

"Prijntgen Van der Velde jonge dochter mede van Leyden vergeselschapt met moeychen Tay haer moeder."

(The English Translation)

"John Telly, say-weaver, singleman of Leyden, accompanied by Paul Telly his father,

with

"Prijntgen Van der Velde, single woman, also of Leyden, accompanied by Moeychen Tay, her mother."

The use of the terms "Jongman" meaning single man, or bachelor, and "Jong dochter," meaning single woman, proves that neither "Jan Telly" nor "Prijntgen Van der Velde" had ever been married before.

Mr. Bowman, a careful historian, has advanced the following reasoning:

Elizabeth Tilley came in the "Mayflower" with her father, John Tilley, and later married John Howland. The date of her marriage is unknown but her son John[2] Howland, born February 24, 1626/27 *(Judge Sewall's Diary)* and her daughter Desire[2] Howland whose birth date is unknown, were both living in 22 May 1627. Unless these children were twins, which seems unlikely from the meager data obtainable, Desire must have been born as early as February 1625/6. Whether or not they were twins, it is certain that on 24 February 1626/7, Elizabeth (Tilley) Howland was the mother of two children. In her will dated 17 December 1686, she called herself "Seventy-nine years of age but of good and perfect memory," thus fixing her own birth date as about 1607 or 1608. As the statement of the will is supported by the known facts regarding her children, and nothing has been found which casts any doubt upon it, we must accept it as correct. But even if we did not have the statement of the will by which to fix the age of Elizabeth Tilley, it is evident that she must have been born before March 3, 1615, otherwise she would have become the mother of two children before she was twelve years of age. Since Elizabeth (Tilley) Howland was born before March 3rd, 1615, she could not have been a daughter either of "Jan Tellij" or of "Prijntgen Van der Velde" who were married on that date neither having been married before.

The only known contemporary references to the parentage of Elizabeth (Tilley) Howland are found in Bradford's "History." In the list of "Mayflower" passengers he mentions her three times as follows:

"John Tillie, and his wife, and Elizabeth their daughter," *(B 408)*.

"John Howland married the daughter of John Tillie, Elizabeth, and they are both now living," *(B 410)*.

"John Tillie and his wife both dyed a little after they came ashore; and their daughter, Elizabeth married with John Howland," *(B 412)*.

These statements were written by Governor Bradford while John Howland and his wife were still living in

Plymouth, where all three had lived for more than thirty years and Bradford must then have had his own manuscript "register . . . recording some of the first deaths, marriages and punishments," which Rev. Thomas Prince obtained from the Governor's Grandson, Major John Bradford, and referred to so frequently in his "New England Chronology," published in 1736. Governor Bradford was in a position to know the facts. Therefore, as no evidence has yet been produced to contradict his statements, we must accept them as they have come down to us in his own handwriting.

It has been shown that Elizabeth (Tilley) Howland was not the daughter of "Jan Tellij," the Leyden bridegroom of 1615, and on the other hand it has been shown that she was the daughter of John Tilley of the "Mayflower." It is evident therefore, that "Jan Tellij" and John Tilley were not identical, but were two entirely distinct individuals. *(M.D. X 65-67) (M.D. XXIII 76)*.

86—*Elizabeth (Comyngs) Tilley* has been tentatively identified as the wife of John Tilley. She came with her husband and daughter *(B 408)*. For many years her daughter Elizabeth, wife of John Howland, was supposed to be a daughter of Governor Carver until Governor Bradford's "History" showed this was untrue. John Tilley and his wife were the parents of Elizabeth *(B 87) (MD I 10) (MD X 65) (MD XXIII 76)*, whose name immediately follows.

87—*Elizabeth* [2] *Tilley* came with her parents *(B 408)*. For many years because of family tradition she was thought to be a daughter of Governor Carver until Governor Bradford's history was discovered *(T 129)*. The tradition arose because she was treated by Carver as a daughter. She married John Howland. After his death she went to live with her daughter, Lydia, who had married James Brown and was living in Rehoboth. When she made her will, she was of Swansea. She died December 31, 1687, and was buried in the Brown lot in the Little Neck Cemetery now Riverside, Rhode Island. Her will is published *(MD III 54)*

156

(Bristol County Probate Records, Vol. I, pg. 13-14). She and John have had many descendants *(MI)*.

88—*Thomas Tinker* came with his wife and son *(B 408)*. He was the nineteenth signer of the Mayflower Compact. He was born in 1581, at Thurne, County Norfolk, England, and became a carpenter at Neatishead, County Norfolk, England. He is credited to the Leyden contingent. *(BK 89)*. The name of his wife is unknown. He died at Plymouth between January 11 and April 10, 1621, in the first general sickness *(MD II 119)*. He left no known descendants.

89—*Mrs. Tinker* came with her husband and son *(B 408)*. She died at Plymouth after January 11, early in 1621, in the first general sickness *(MD II 119)*. She left no known descendants.

90—   *Tinker,* son of Thomas and wife, came with his parents *(B 408)*. This son died at Plymouth in the first general sickness after January 11, early in 1621 *(MD II 119)*. His first name is unknown.

91—*William Trevore* was a seaman who was hired to stay a year in the New World. He was undoubtedly employed because of his previous experience and knowledge of the New England coast obtained as one of the crew of Captain Dermer's ship the year previously *(BK 90)*. He did not sign the Mayflower Compact, probably because he did not intend to remain. After his time had expired, he returned to England. He came over thereafter as master of a ship. His previous voyages are described in a deposition made by him *(BK 90)*. A letter written by Robert Cushman in England to Governor William Bradford in Plymouth mentions a proposed plantation, to be made by Thomas Weston, as follows: "It is like he will plant to the southward of the Cape, for William Trevore hath lavishly tould but what he knew or imagined of Capewack, Mohiggen, and the Narigansets." *(B 136)*. He died without known descendants after May 7, 1650 *(MD II 119)*.

92—*John Turner* came with two sons. A daughter came

later to Salem and married there *(B 408)*. He is mentioned by Robert Cushman in a letter dated June 11, 1620, to the bretheren in Leyden *(B 74)*. He was the twenty-second signer of the Mayflower Compact and is classed with the Leyden contingent. He was probably the one who in 1592 sold a messuage in Doncaster, England, and may be the one who was married at Whitechapel in 1615 *(BK 91)*. He died at Plymouth during the first general sickness between January 11 and April 10, 1621. *(MD II 119)*. He left no known descendants.

93—   *Turner* came with his father and brother *(B 408)*. His first name is unknown. He died at Plymouth in the first general sickness after January 11, early in 1621 *(MD II 119)*.

94—   *Turner* came with his father and brother *(B 408)*. His first name also is unknown. He died at Plymouth after January 11, early in 1621, in the first general sickness *(MD II 120)*.

95—*Mr. Richard Warren* came alone. His wife and five daughters were left behind and came afterwards on the "Anne" *(B 408)*. He was the twelfth signer of the Mayflower Compact. He married before 1611, Elizabeth, whose last name is unknown and who was born about 1583. He was from London. He was a member of the third expedition which left the "Mayflower" in the shallop on December 16 and was in the First Encounter with the Indians on December 18. This party eventually landed on the rock and selected Plymouth as their new home *(MR 43)*, *(B 9)*. He was among the "Purchasers" of 1627 to buy from the London adventurers all their rights to the colony. *(MD III 45)*. He stood at the head of the ninth share in the division of cattle in 1627. His location of lands was near Eel River, and the land remained in the possession of his descendants for many years *(T 70-71)*. He died at Plymouth in 1628. His wife died at Plymouth October 12, 1673 *(MD II 120)* *(MD III 50)*. They have had many descendants *(N.E., Vol.*

55, pp. 70-78, 161-170) (MI), including two Presidents of the United States, Ulysses S. Grant and Franklin Delano Roosevelt. The latter is descended from him in five lines. Other descendants have been Colonel Benjamin Church, the Indian fighter; the Reverend Josiah Cotton, Harvard, 1698; James Warren, President of the Continental Congress; Dr. Charles Thomas Jackson, scientist; Dr. Cyrus Briggs, Harvard, 1821, famous surgeon; Charlemagne Tower, former Ambassador to Germany; John Bartlett, author of Bartlett's "Familiar Quotations"; Major General Frederick Dent Grant, distinguished soldier and his son, Major General Ulysses S. Grant, 3rd; Major General Leonard Wood, commander of the "Rough Riders" and later of the American Army in Cuba; George W. Baker, the philanthropist; and Governor Robert Bradford of Massachusetts. Among the women descended from him is Louise Dutton Fillmore, the authoress, who comes from him in two lines, and also Mrs. Ralph Waldo Emerson.

96—*Mr. William White* came with his wife and one son Resolved. Another son Peregrine was born on the "Mayflower." He brought two servants, William Holbeck and Edward Thomson *(B 408)*. He was the eleventh signer of the Mayflower Compact and was one of the Leyden contingent *(BK 94-95)*. He married at Leyden, Holland, February 11, 1612, Susanna Fuller *(MD VII 193-194)*. He died at Plymouth March 3, 1621, during the first general sickness. His widow married Edward Winslow *(MD II 120)*. He has left many descendants. *(Thomas and Samuel White's "Descendants of William White") (MI)*.

97—*Susanna (Fuller) White* came with her husband and son, and had another son Peregrine born on the "Mayflower" *(B 408)*. She had married William White at Leyden, Holland, on February 11, 1612 *(MD VII 193-194)*. After his death at Plymouth on March 3, 1621, she married Edward Winslow at Plymouth on May 22, 1621 *(MD II 120)*.

98—*Resolved* ² *White* came with his parents *(B 408)*. He

married first, November 15, 1640, Judith Vassall, daughter of William Vassall. She was buried at Marshfield, April 13, 1670. He married, second, at Salem Massachusetts, October 15, 1674, Abigail (   ) Lord, widow of William Lord. She died at Salem, between June 25 and July 7, 1682. He died between 1690 and 1694. *(MD II 120)*. He has had many descendants.

99—*Peregrine* ² *White* was born on the "Mayflower" at Cape Cod Harbor between December 7 and 10, 1620 *(HX I 27)*. He volunteered for the Pequot War in 1636 and was an ensign during the Narragansett troubles in 1642. He was later a captain and a member of the Council of War in 1675. He married before March 16, 1649, Sarah Bassett, daughter of William Bassett. He died at Marshfield July 31, 1704. His will has been published *(MD I 129)*. The inventory has also been published *(MD VIII 119)* (Plymouth Probate Records Book, Vol. 2, pg. 48). His widow died at Marshfield, February 2, 1712 *(MD II 120)*. He left many descendants.

100—*Roger Wilder* came as a servant of John Carver *(B 407)*. He did not sign the Mayflower Compact. He died at Plymouth between January 11 and April 12, 1621, during the first general sickness *(MD II 120)*. He left no known descendants.

101—*Thomas Williams* came alone *(B 409)*. He came from Yarmouth, County Norfolk, and had lived in Leyden with his sister *(BK 97)*. He was the thirtieth signer of the Mayflower Compact. He died at Plymouth between January 11, and April 10, 1621 *(MD II 120)*, during the first general sickness. Bradford states that he died soon after landing, *(B 413)* yet attempts have been made to prove that he did not die. The Society of Mayflower Descendants has accepted no alleged descendants from him.

102—*Mr. Edward Winslow* came with his wife and two servants George Soule and Elias Story *(B 407)*. He was the third signer of the Mayflower Compact. He was born at

Droitwich, Worcestershire, England, on October 28, 1595. He married, first, at Leyden, May 16, 1618, Elizabeth Barker of Chester, England *(MD VIII 100) (R 213)*. She came with him on the "Mayflower" but died during the first general sickness in Plymouth on April 3, 1621. He married, second, at Plymouth, on May 22, 1621, Susanna, widow of William White, who had also died during the first sickness. This was the first marriage ever solemnized in New England. He was one of the company which, in the shallop, first explored the shores of Cape Cod, engaged in the First Encounter at Eastham and which proceeded thence to Plymouth harbor and reached Clark's Island in great distress *(M 31)*. He was one of those who first landed and selected Plymouth as the place of settlement *(MR 43)*. When Massasoit made his first appearance on Strawberry Hill, inviting an interview with the settlers, "Winslow was deputed to meet him and he voluntarily placed himself as hostage in the hands of the Indians while their chief, Massasoit, held his interview with Governor Carver." In July, 1621, he and Stephen Hopkins *(M 48)* "were appointed to visit Massasoit, at his cabin at Pokanoket, for the purpose of exploring the country, and ascertaining the situation, character, and strength of the tribe, and to cultivate their friendship." In the month of March, 1623, with John Hampden, he was again dispatched to visit Massasoit when the latter was dangerously sick, and Winslow was the fortunate means of restoring him to health when apparently about expiring. In September, 1623, Winslow was dispatched to England on the "Ann," as an agent, to transact business for the Colony, and, in the short space of six months, he returned in March, 1624, on the ship "Charity," bringing provisions, clothing, and the first stock of cattle ever in New England. While in England he published a narrative, entitled "Good News from New England, or A Relation of Things Remarkable in That Plantation." During 1630, he was again sent to England as agent for the Colony. In the year 1625 he was elected one of the five assistants in the colonial government in which office he continued until 1633. In the latter year, Governor Bradford having served about twelve years asked that someone take his place, and as a result Edward Winslow was that year chosen third Governor of the Colony. At a general court held October 28, 1633, it was agreed that the chief government should be held in the town of Plymouth, and that the governor live there and keep his residence and dwelling there and also hold meetings of the court there. (T 74). This meant that Winslow was obliged to live in Plymouth rather than in Marshfield, where he had lived since 1638 on his pretentious estate "Careswell." The next year he was again chosen one of the assistants, which office he filled for eleven years. In 1635, he accepted another mission to England, jointly for the Colonies of Plymouth and Massachusetts. It was during this mission that he was persecuted by Archbishop Laud for speaking in Church and for solemnizing marriages as a magistrate and was committed to Fleet Prison, where he remained seventeen weeks before he was released. When he returned to Plymouth in 1636, he was again elected Governor but the year following became one of the magistrates. In 1643, he was Plymouth commissioner in the newly formed confederated New England Colonies and held the office for three years. In 1644, he served again as Governor. In 1646, he went to England for the fourth time and did not return. At that visit through his influence the Society of the Propagation of the Gospel among the Indians was established in 1649, and it is still in existence. He published "Hypocrisie Unmasked" (London 1646), and the next year published "New England's Salamander." He was in high favor with Oliver Cromwell and his officers and was invited to accept employment in Cromwell's service. In 1654, he received the appointment of first commissioner to arbitrate and determine the value of the English ships seized and detained by the King of Denmark in 1652. His last public service was when in 1655 he received from Cromwell the appointment of commissioner, with Admiral Penn and General Venable, to capture the Spanish West Indies and to govern Hispaniola. On the passage to attack Jamaica, he became ill of fever and died. His remains were buried at sea on May 8, 1655, with the honors of war and a forty-two gun salute. *(T 88-94) (B 117 note) (MD V 224-233)*. He left a will *(MD IV 1)* (Somerset House Records, London). He has had descendants *(WT) (N.E., Vol. 17, pp. 159-162) (MI)*, many of whom have been described herein at length.

103—*Elizabeth (Barker) Winslow* came with her husband *(B 407)*. She was from Chester, Suffolk, England. She died at Plymouth in the first general sickness on April 3, 1621. *(MD II 120)*.

104—*Gilbert Winslow* was born on November 5, 1600, at Droitwich, Worcestershire, England. He was a younger brother of Edward Winslow. He came alone and was the thirty-first signer of the Mayflower Compact. Bradford says of him "after diverse years aboad here, returned to England, and dyed ther" *(B 413)*. He returned to England about 1626 and died in 1650. *(HX II 30) (MD II 120)*. He left no known descendants.

APPENDIX B

COMPACT SIGNED IN THE CABIN
OF THE "MAYFLOWER"

IN YE NAME OF GOD, AMEN.—WE whose names are underwriten, the loyall subjects of our dread soveraigne Lord, King James, by yᵉ grace of God, of Great Britaine, Franc, & Ireland King, Defender of yᵉ Faith, &c.

Haveing under-taken, for yᵉ glorie of God, and advancemente of yᵉ Christian faith and honour of our King & Countrie, a voyage to plant yᵉ first colonie in yᵉ northerne parts of Virginia, doe by these presents solemnly & mutualy in yᵉ presence of God, and one of another, covenant, & combine our selves together into a civill body politick, for our better ordering, preservation, & furtherance of yᵉ ends aforesaid; and by vertue hereof to enacte, constitute, and frame shuch just & equall lawes, ordinances, acts, constitutions & offices, from time to time, as shall be thought most meete & convenient for yᵉ generall good of yᵉ Colonie; unto which we promise all due submission and obedience.

IN WITNESS WHEREOF we have hereunder subscribed our name at Cap-codd yᵉ 11 of November, in yᵉ year of yᵉ raigne of our soveraigne Lord King James of England, France & Ireland yᵉ eighteenth, and of Scotland yᵉ fiftie fourth, Anᵒ Dom. 1620 *(B 107).*

The foregoing has been copied from Bradford's "History." What follows has been copied from Morton's "New

England Memorial," 1669 edition, in which there are three columns of seven names each at the bottom of a page:

John Carver	Samuel Fuller	Edward Tilley
William Bradford	Christopher Martin	John Tilley
Edward Winslow	William Mullins	Francis Cooke
William Brewster	William White	Thomas Rogers
Isaac Allerton	Richard Warren	Thomas Tinker
John Alden	John Howland	John Ridgdale
Myles Standish	Stephen Hopkins	Edward Fuller

At the top of the following page the names appear as follows:

John Turner	Degory Priest	Richard Gardiner
Francis Eaton	Thomas Williams	Richard Clarke
James Chilton	Gilbert Winslow	John Allerton
John Crackston	Edmund Margeson	Thomas English
John Billington	Peter Brown	Edward Doty
Moses Fletcher	Richard Britteridge	Edward Leister
John Goodman	George Soule	*(MD I 79)*.

APPENDIX C

What Later Generations Have Said Concerning the Pilgrims

"HISTORY OF PLYMOUTH COLONY"

Francis Baylies, 1830, Page 30:

"On the bleak shore of a barren wilderness, in the midst of desolation, with the blasts of winter howling around them, and surrounded with dangers in their most awful and appalling forms, the Pilgrims of Leyden laid the foundations of American Liberty."

"DOCUMENTS OF AMERICAN HISTORY"

- edited by Howard Preston:

"The Compact appears as the First American State Paper. The commentary contains a quotation from the historian, George Bancroft: 'Here was the birth of popular constitutional liberty — In the cabin of the Mayflower, Humanity recovered its rights, and instituted government on the basis of equal laws enacted by all the people for the general good.'"

"THE PILGRIMS"
Frederic A. Noble—Boston, 1907, Page 197:

"The Mayflower Compact is an immortal document. It is justly counted one of the most important contributions ever made to the civic thought of the world. The tender reverence in which it ought to be read will be increased if we remember that of the forty-one who affixed their names to it, twenty were dead before the end of the following March." On Page 198: "Goldwin Smith says: 'It heralded a policy of self-government, and may rank among the great documents of history.'" On Page 199: "Those obscure statesmen down in the cabin of the Mayflower were beginning to write, and to teach the World to write Man with a capital letter."

"THE FOUNDING OF NEW ENGLAND"
James Truslow Adams, 1927, Page 98:

"The Compact remained the only basis on which the independent civil government in Plymouth rested, as the colonists were never able to get a charter conferring rights of jurisdiction. It was the first example of that 'plantation covenant' which was to form the basis of the river towns of Connecticut, of New Haven, and of so many other towns or colony governments."

"THE AMERICAN CANON"
Daniel L. Marsh, President, Boston University, 1909.

Among his Seven Canons of American Democracy (there is no eighth), he put the Compact first: "The Genesis of American Democracy is in the Mayflower Compact."

"HISTORY OF THE PILGRIMS AND PURITANS"
K. D. Sawyer, 1922., Vol. II, Page 4:

"A document equal in value to Doomsday Book or Magna Charter has been written and will be signed. Destiny presides at the board and unknown to themselves the makers of a great nation here hold converse." On Page 8, he quotes Goldsmith as saying: "The roll of Battle Abbey is a poor record beside it." Also he quotes Pres. John Q. Adams as saying: "The Compact is perhaps the only

167

instance in human history of that positive, original social compact, which speculative philosophers have imagined as the only legitimate source of government." On Page 9: "The Compact obliterated both feudalism and ecclesiasticism."

"THE PILGRIMS AND THEIR MONUMENT"
Edmund J. Carpenter.
Cambridge, 1911. Pp. 183 and 184

"From the Compact was to spring not only a stable government for the little colony, but a great series of Constitutions for free states. They started on this Continent the practise of electing, by manhood suffrage, the head of a state, for a limited period. It was a small beginning, but who can comprehend or describe the immensity of the outcome."

"THE MAYFLOWER PILGRIMS"
Edmund J. Carpenter, 1920, Page 79

"The Compact is one of the most important acts known to history." P. 80: "Here was the germ root of our great Republic: the first charter of a government for the people and by the people known to history. This historic occurrence is the subject of one of the great paintings in the Rotunda of the Capitol at Washington. It is also commemorated, as a notable occurrence in English History, in a splendid mural painting in the Houses of Parliament in London."

"THE PILGRIM FATHERS"
Winnifred Cockshott, 1909, Page 195

"By this step, which recognized the settlers themselves as the real source of power, the Pilgrims had, for all practical purposes, made themselves politically independent: and, as the colony was remote, and England, for many years to come, was occupied with troubles of her own, this independence and the form of government which it dictated, were never seriously interfered with."

INTRODUCTION TO "CHRONICALES*OF THE PILGRIM FATHERS," IN EVERYMAN'S LIBRARY
John Masefield, 1910

"A generation fond of pleasure, disinclined towards serious thought, and shrinking from hardship, even if it may be swiftly reached, will find it difficult to imagine the temper, courage and manliness of the emigrants who made the first Christian settlement in New England."

"TRAVELS THROUGH NEW ENGLAND"
Volume II, Page 110
Rev. Timothy Dwight, President of Yale College, 1795 to 1816

"Plymouth was the first town built in New England by civilized men; and those by whom it was built were inferior in worth to no body of men whose names are recorded in history during the last 1700 years. A kind of venerableness, arising from these facts, attaches to this town, which may be termed a prejudice. Still, it has its foundation in the nature of man, and will never be eradicated either by philosophy or ridicule. No New-Englander, who is willing to indulge his native feelings, can stand upon the rock where our ancestors set the first foot after their arrival on the American shore, without experiencing emotions very different from those which are excited by any common object of the same nature. No New Englander would be willing to have that rock buried and forgotten. Let him reason, as much, as coldly, and as ingenuously as he pleases, he will still regard that spot with emotions wholly different from those which are excited by other places of equal or even superior importance."

*See page 196.

DANIEL WEBSTER
From his bi-Centennial address at Plymouth,
Forefathers' Day, 1820

"Forever honored be this, the place of our fathers' refuge. Forever remembered the day which saw them, weary and distressed, broken in everything but spirit, poor in all but faith and courage, at last secure from the dangers of wintry seas, and impressing this shore with the first footsteps of civilized men.

"We have come to this Rock, to record here our homage for our Pilgrim Fathers; our sympathy in their sufferings; our gratitude for their labors; our admiration of their virtues; our veneration for their piety; and our attachment to those principles of civil and religious liberty, for which they encountered the dangers of the ocean, the storms of heaven, the violence of savages, disease, exile and famine, to enjoy and to establish.

"The first scene of our history was laid on this spot. Here Christianity and civilization and letters made their first lodgement, in a vast extent of country, covered with a wilderness, and peopled by roving barbarians. Thanks be to God that this spot was honored as the asylum of religious liberty. May its standard, reared here, remain forever. May it rise up as high as heaven, till its banner shall fan the air of both continents, and wave as a glorious ensign of peace and security to the nations.

"At the moment of their landing they possessed institutions of government and of religion; they were a group of friends and families, knit together by social bonds, established by consent; founded on choice and preference. How nearly do these fill up our whole idea of country. Here they were, on the shore of a rude and fearful winderness, unprotected and unprovided for; yet politic, intelligent, and educated.

"They established, in the forest, institutions containing,

in substance, all that the ages had evolved. Cultivated mind was to act on uncultivated nature; and, more than all, a government and a country were to commence, with the very first foundations laid under the divine light of the Christian religion. Our first breath, the inspirations of liberty. This was our origin. Happy auspices of a happy future.

"We cannot well over-rate the responsibility and duty which these blessings impose upon us. These institutions are to be transmitted, as well as enjoyed. We are in the line of conveyance, through which whatever has been obtained by the spirit and efforts of our ancestors, is to be communicated to our children.

"We are bound to maintain public liberty, and by the example of our own systems, to convince the world, that order and law, religion and morality, the rights of conscience, the rights of persons, and the rights of property, may all be preserved and secured, in the most perfect manner, by a government entirely and purely elective.

"Advance, then, ye future generations. We would hail you, as you rise, in your long succession, to fill the places which we now fill, and to taste the blessings of existence, where we are passing, and soon shall have passed, our own human duration. We bid you welcome to the pleasant land of the Fathers. We greet your accession to the great inheritance which we have enjoyed. We welcome you to the immeasurable blessings of rational existence, the immortal hope of Christianity, and the light of everlasting Truth."

THE VOYAGE OF THE MAYFLOWER
From the Oration Delivered at Plymouth
December 22, 1824, by Edward Everett

"I see it now; that one, solitary, adventurous vessel, the Mayflower, of a forlorn hope; freighted with the prospects of a future State, and bound across the unknown sea. I behold it pursuing, with a thousand misgivings, the uncertain, the tedious voyage. Suns rise and set; the weeks and months pass, and Winter surprises them on the deep, but brings them not the sight of the wished-for shore.

"I see them; crowded, almost to suffocation, in their ill-stored prison; delayed by calms, pursuing a circuitous route; and now driven by the fury of the raging tempest, on the high and giddy waves. The awful voice of the storm howls through the rigging. The laboring masts seem straining from their base. The dismal sound of the pumps is heard. The ship leaps, madly from billow to billow. The ocean breaks, and settles, with engulfing floods, over the floating deck, and beats with shivering, shattering force, against the staggering vessel.

"I see them, escaped from these perils, still pursuing their all but desperate undertaking; landed at last, after three months passage, on the ice-clad Rock of Plymouth; weak and weary from the voyage; poorly armed; scantily provisioned; without shelter; without means; in the grip of pestilence; surrounded by hostile tribes.

"Shut now the volume of history, and tell me, on any principle of human probability; what shall be the fate of this handful of adventurers? Tell me, man of military science, how soon were they all swept off by the thirty savage tribes, enumerated within the early limits of New England? Tell me, politician, how long did this shadow of a colony, on which your conventions and treaties had not smiled, languish on that distant coast? Student of history, compare for me the baffled projects, the deserted settlements, the abandoned adventures of other times, AND FIND THE PARALLEL OF THIS!

"Was it the Winter's storms, beating on the houseless heads of women and children; was it hard labor and spare meals; was it disease; was it the tomahawk; was it the deep malady of a blighted hope, a ruined enterprise, and a broken heart, aching in its last moments, at the recollection

172

of the loved and left, beyond the sea; was it some, or all of these united, that hurried this forsaken company to their melancholy fate?

"And is it possible that not one of these causes; that not all combined, were able to blast this bud of hope? Is it possible, that from a beginning so feeble, so frail, so worthy, not so much of admiration as of pity; there has gone forth a progress so steady, a growth so wonderful, a reality so important, a promise, Yet To Be Fulfilled, SO GLORIOUS?"

ROBERT C. WINTHROP, 1839
From his oration before the New England Society
of New York at the Broadway Tabernacle

"The Pilgrim settlement exerted a paramount influence on the early destinies of this Continent, and gave the first unequivocal assurance that virtue and industry and freedom were here to find a refuge and here to found themselves an empire.

"A feeble company of exiles, quitting the strange land to which persecution had forced them to flee. Entering with so many sighs and sobs and partings and prayers, on a voyage so full of perils at the best, but rendered a hundred fold more perilous by the unusual severities of the season and the un-sea-worthiness of their ship.

"Arriving in the depth of winter, on a coast to which even their pilot was a perfect stranger, and where famine, exposure, the wolf, the savage, disease and death seemed waiting for them. Yet accomplishing an end which Royalty and patronage, the love of dominion and of gold, individual adventure and corporate enterprise had so long essayed in vain.

"Founding a Colony which was to defy alike the machinations and the menaces of Tyranny, in all periods of its history. Higher than human was the Power which presided over the Exodus of the Pilgrim Fathers.

"Conscience was the nearest to an earthly power which the Pilgrims possessed, and freedom of Conscience the nearest to an earthly motive which prompted their career.

"It was Conscience which emboldened them to launch their fragile bark upon a merciless ocean, fearless of the fighting winds and lowering storms.

"It was Conscience which stiffened them to brave the perils, endure the hardships, undergo the deprivations of a howling, houseless, hopeless desolation.

"It was Conscience, inspiring a courage, confirming a resolution, and accomplishing an enterprise, of which the records of the world will be searched in vain to find a parallel."

RUFUS CHOATE
From his oration before the New England Society
of New York, Forefathers' Day, 1843

"It is a great thing for a nation to be able to look to an authentic race of founders and an historical principle of institution, in which it may admire the realized idea of true heroism. It is a great and precious thing to be able to ascend to an heroic age and an heroic race which it may call its own. An heroic age and race, the extent and permanence of whose influences are of a kind to kindle the moral imagination and justify the intelligent wonder of the world. Freedom hovered over the rock-bound coast of New England and set the Stars of Glory there.

"To found a state upon a waste of earth, wherein great numbers of human beings may live together, and in successive generations, socially and in peace; knit to one-another by innumerable ties, light as air, yet stronger than links of iron, which compose the national existence,—wherein they may help each other, and be helped in bearing the various lots of life,—wherein they may enjoy and improve, and impart and heighten enjoyment and improvement,— wherein they may together perform the real social labors, may reclaim and decorate the earth, may disinter the treasures that grow beneath its surface; may invent and polish the arts of usefulness and beauty; may perfect the loftier arts of virtue and empire, open and work the richer minds of the universal youthful heart and intellect, and spread out a dwelling for the Muse on the glittering summits of Freedom;—to found such a State is the first of heroical labors and heroical glories.

"The Pilgrims were moved by a thirst for freedom from unnecessary restraint, which is tyranny,—freedom of the soul, freedom of thought, a larger measure of freedom of life. These were the motives, from which the current of our national fortunes has issued forth. You can look around you today, and see into how broad and deep a stream that current has expanded; what accumulations of costly and beautiful things it bears along; through what valley of happiness and rest it rolls towards some mightier sea.

"Silently adopted was the grand doctrine that all men are born equal and born free—born to the same inheritance exactly of chances and of hopes; that every child ought to be equally with every other, invited and stimulated to strive for the happiest life, the largest future, the most conspicuous virtue, the fullest mind, the brightest wreath. How skillfully these have been adapted to the nature of things and the needs of men; how well the principle of permanence has been harmonized with the principle of progress.

"From all this rich heritage, a wise, moral and glorious future should evolve. These heroic men and women should not look down on a dwindled posterity. We take from them in whom the loftiest sense of duty blended itself with the fiercest spirit of liberay.[*] Yet, our past is nothing, but as you, quickened by its examples, warned by its voices, shall reproduce it in the life of today. Its once busy existence, fiery trials, dear-bought triumphs; its dynasty of heroes, all its pulses of joy and anguish, hopes and fears, love and praise, are now with the years beyond the flood. Yet, gazing

*See page 196.

on these, long and intently and often, we may pass into the likeness of the departed,—may emulate their labors, and partake of their immortality."

CHARLES SUMNER
From his oration on the Embarkation Anniversary,
Plymouth. August 1, 1853

"The Pilgrims were among the earliest of Separatists. As such, they knew, by bitter experience, all the sharpness of persecution. Against them the men in power raged like the heathen. Against them the whole fury of the law was directed. Some were imprisoned; all were impoverished. For safety and freedom the little band sought shelter in Holland, where they continued in indigence and obscurity for more than ten years, when they were inspired to seek a home in this unknown Western world.

"By a covenant with the Lord, they had vowed to walk in all His ways, according to their best endeavors, whatsoever it should cost them. Repentance and prayers; patience and tears were their weapons. Self-sacrifice is never in vain, and they foresaw, with clearness of phophecy, that out of their trials should come a transcendent future. Governor Bradford said: 'As one small candle may light a thousand, so the light here kindled in some sort shrine, even to the whole nation.' *

"These are the men whom we have met in this goodly number to celebrate; not for any victory of war; not for any triumph of discovery, science, learning or eloquence; not for worldly success of any kind. How poor are all these things by the side of that divine virtue which made them, amidst the reproach, the obloquy, and the harshness of the world, hold fast to Freedom and to Truth.

"Plymouth Rock is the imperishable symbol that shall forever proclaim their deviation from received opinions, their self-sacrifice, their un-quenchable thirst for Liberty. We see clearly what it has done for the world, and what it

*See page 196.

has done for their fame. From gushing, multitudinous hearts we now thank these lowly men that they dared to be true and brave. In vindication of a cherished principle, they stood alone, against the madness of men, against the law of the land, even against their King. They won the battle for human freedom; therefore they will be enshrined in the hearts of all true men till time shall be no more."

* * * * *

These stirring words aroused the Nation anew to a sense of its debt to the Pilgrims, which was finally expressed in the magnificent monument to the Forefathers in Plymouth.

WILLIAM M. EVARTS
From his oration before the New England Society
of New York, Forefathers' Day, 1854

"Upon the Rock of Plymouth was pressed the first footstep of that energetic and creative power in human affairs which has since over-run this Continent. Through the scene of debarkation, made up of wintry sea and gloomy sky, and bleak and desolate coast, we see breaking the light and hope which have ever since shone bright as the source of those radiant glories of freedom in whose glad light we live; warm with the fervent glow of that beneficent activity which pervades and invigorates the life of this whole nation; which has secured the progress of the past, and forms the hope of the future.

"The Pilgrims never valued liberty as an end. But, as a means to duty, it was dearer than life itself. They sought it only that they might subject themselves to a more thorough discipline. Loyalty to a ruler they replaced by obedience to law. They threw off the yoke of their king only to pursue the stricter service of their God. The fair flower of liberty they watered with their tears and with their blood, but only that they might feed upon its sober fruit, Duty.

"In their enterprise, the culture and development of the individual was the controlling object. It recognized the

177

brotherhood of all men; raising them to the very threshold of heaven. In their establishment of the Christian faith upon this un-peopled Continent, the Pilgrims were the bearers of a new mission, than which there had been none greater since the time of the Apostles.

"They established liberty and law; civilization and religion; for a habitation to posterity to the latest generation. If we are guided by the same high motives, imbued with the same deep wisdom, warmed with the same faithful spirit as were they; no evil however great, can withstand us; no peril, however dark, can dismay us."

WILLIAM T. DAVIS
From his oration on the Two Hundred and Fiftieth Anniversary of the Landing of the Pilgrims, Plymouth, December 21, 1870

"The battle-field on which you have this day trod is more sacred than any other which history records. The decisive battles of the world sink into insignificance beside the battle which our Fathers fought along the hillside and round the Rock of Plymouth. No armed hosts, with shining helmet and waving plume met here in battle array; no trumpet sounded the charge; no warrior's lance or bristling steel met the opposing foe; no royal hand crowned the victorious chief. No new division of regal power, no readjustment of imperial lines, no fate of potentate or prince, depended on the issue.

"But in the battle a new civilization asserted its claim against the insolent pretentions of the old; the rights of man stood up against the domination of kings; the human conscience fought to free itself from the shackles of servitude. This was the battle which our Fathers fought; and neither hunger nor hardship, nor the terrible uncertainties of the future, nor the allurements of their distant home, nor pestilence nor death, could check their courage or shake their faith.

"With the battle still raging, ay, well-nigh lost; with one-half their number sleeping in their graves, — they sent their only refuge back across the seas, and sought, with a serene confidence, the guidance and protection of their God. A brighter page and a sweeter song shall proclaim to nations yet unborn, as the noblest typification of faith in God, that sublime incident in Christian history, the return of the Mayflower to England.

"Welcome to this hallowed field. Inhale, with fullest breath, the atmosphere of this sacred spot. Drink long and deep at this fountain of our Nation's greatness. Go back to your homes with the vow recorded in your hearts to make yourselves worthier of this heritage. Let us remember that fidelity to duty—duty to ourselves, to our country and to our God—will be the noblest monument that we can rear in memory of the virtue and the sacrifices of the Pilgrims."

GEORGE WILLIAM CURTIS

From his oration at the Dedication of the Statue
"The Pilgrim" by J. Q. A. Ward, Central Park,
New York, June 6, 1885

"The Pilgrim emigration to America is a story of achievement unparalleled in the annals of the world for the majesty of its purpose, the poverty of its means, the weakness of the beginning, and the grandeur of the results.

"Behold the frail settlement at Plymouth, clinging to the bleak edge of America; harassed by Indians, beset by beasts, by disease, by exposure, by death in every form; beyond civilization and succor, beyond the knowledge or interest of mankind. Yet taking such a vital hold that it swiftly overspreads and dominates a continent, covered today with a population more industrious, more intelligent, happier, man for man, than any people upon which the sun has ever shone.

"The winds that blew the Mayflower over the sea were

not more truly airs from heaven than the moral impulse and the moral heroism which inspired her voyage.

"Banished by the pitiless English persecution, exiles and poor in a foreign land, before they were a colony in America, they were compelled to self-government, to a common sympathy and support, to bearing one another's burdens. So, by the stern experience of actual life, they were trained in the virtues most essential for the fulfillment of their august but unimagined destiny.

"Here, in this sylvan seclusion, we raise the statue of the Pilgrim, that in this changeless form, the long procession of the generations which follow us, may see what manner of man he was who walked, undismayed, the solitary, heights of duty and of everlasting service to mankind. Here let him stand, the builder of a free state, serenely confronting the continent which he shall settle and subdue.

"The unspeaking lips shall chide our unworthiness, the lofty mien exalt our littleness, the unblenching eye invigorate our weakness; and the whole poised and firmly planted form reveal the unconquerable moral energy—the masterforce of American civilization. So may our Nation stand, forever and forever, the mighty guardian of human liberty, of God-like justice, of Christ-like brotherhood."

HON. EDWIN D. MEAD, 1893

"There is no other church in which all New Englanders and all Americans feel a sense of possession, of which all are in a manner members, to the extent which is true of the First Church in Plymouth. We forget all creeds and all changes of creeds; we care little what preacher is in the pulpit or what title is on the hymn-book, what title was there yesterday or what title will be there tomorrow. We remember only that this was the church of the Mayflower congregation and of Elder Brewster, the church of Bradford and Carver and Winslow, the church of the pioneers sent into the New England wilderness by John Robinson with the charge never to 'come to a period in religion,' but ever to keep their minds open for 'more light and truth.' It was the first purely democratic church in modern times, which means that it was the first purely democratic church in history. It was the church of the men who signed the compact on the Mayflower, that great first word in the history of American liberty and independence. The signers would have found it hard, many of them, to tell whether they signed it in their capacity as members of the church or as members of the 'civil body politic.' They would have found it hard to the end of their days to tell whether they were doing this and that in their capacity as members of the Church of Christ or as citizens of Plymouth: for they looked upon the end and aim of citizenship and the churchmanship as the same.

"It is the trustee of the great Pilgrim traditions; and its high office is to act with the public to keep the sacred memories fresh and give them power."

GOVERNOR ROGER WOLCOTT
OF MASSACHUETTS
From his address on receiving the Bradford History,
Boston, 1897

"There are places and objects so intimately associated with the world's greatest men or with mighty deeds, that the soul of him who gazes upon them is lost in a sense of reverent awe, as it listens to the voice that speaks from the past.

"On the sloping hillside of Plymouth such a voice is breathed. For here, not alone did godly men and women suffer greatly for a great cause, but their noble purpose was not doomed to defeat, but was carried to perfect victory.

"They established what they planned. Their feeble plantation became the birthplace of religious liberty, the cradle of a free Commonwealth. To them a mighty Nation owes its debt. Nay, they have made the whole world their debtor.

"In the varied tapestry which pictures our national life,

the richest spots are those where gleam the golden threads of conscience, courage and faith, set in the web by that little band.

"May God, in his mercy, grant that the moral impulse, which founded this Nation, may never cease to control its destiny; that no act of any future generation may put in peril the fundamental principles on which it is based: — of equal rights in a free state, equal privileges in a free church and equal opportunities in a free school.

"In this precious volume is told the noble, simple story 'Of Plimoth Plantation.' In the midst of suffering and privation and anxiety, the pious hand of William Bradford has set down the history of the enterprise. May we learn from him: 'that all great and honourable actions are accompanied with great difficulties, and must be both enterprised and overcome with answerable courages.'

"All the sadness and pathos of the narrative are lost in victory. The triumph of a noble cause, even at a great price, is theme for rejoicing, not for sorrow. The story here told is one of triumphant achievement.

"For countless years to come, and to untold thousands, these mute pages shall eloquently speak of high resolve, great suffering and heroic endurance, made possible only by an absolute faith in the overruling providence of Almighty God."

SENATOR GEORGE F. HOAR
From his address at the return of the Bradford Manuscript to Massachusetts. Boston, 1897

"The first American Ambassador to Great Britain comes here to deliver to the lineal successor of Governor Bradford, the only authentic history of the founding of this Commonwealth; the most important political transaction that has ever taken place on the face of the earth.

"Few Americans will gaze upon this manuscript without a little trembling of the lips and a little gathering of mist in the eyes, as they think of the story of suffering, of sorrow, of peril, of exile, of death and of lofty triumph which this book tells, — which the hand of the great leader and founder of America has traced on those pages.

"There is nothing like it in human annals since the story of Bethlehem. These English men and English women going out from their homes in beautiful Lincoln and York, wife separated from husband and mother from child in that hurried embarkation for Holland, pursued to the beach by English horsemen; the thirteen years of exile; the life at Amsterdam 'in alley foul and lane obscure;' the dwelling at Leyden; the embarkation at Delfthaven; the farewell of Robinson; the terrible voyage across the Atlantic; the Compact in the harbor; the landing on the Rock; the dreadful first Winter; the death roll of more than half their number; the days of suffering and famine; the wakeful night, listening for the howl of wild beast and the war-whoop of the savage; the building of the State on those sure foundations which no wave or tempest has ever shaken; the breaking of the new light; the beginning of the new life; the enjoyment of Peace with Liberty, — of all these things, this is the original record by the hand of our beloved father and founder. Massachusetts will forever preserve it."

PRESIDENT CHARLES W. ELIOT
OF HARVARD COLLEGE
From his oration at the Laying of the Cornerstone of the Monument to the Pilgrims, Provincetown, 1910.

"The conceptions and ideals which dominated the lives of the Pilgrims have profoundly influenced the lives of the best part of ten subsequent generations in this Hemisphere. They still exhibit today, under social and industrial conditions very different from those of the 17th century, an abounding and apparently inexhaustible vitality. They held, as a very fruitful conception, that of unlimited progress as the law of human institutions, both civil and religious. This means the progressive discovery and application of Truth to the conduct of human life. They also exhibited a deepseated, comprehensive and inextinguishable love of freedom. The fruits and issues of their pioneering are the most prodigious in all history.

"From the signing of the Compact was to spring not only a stable government for the little Colony, but a great series of Constitutions for Free States. The Pilgrims never accepted a governor appointed by a king. They started, on this Continent the practice of electing the Head of the State, for a limited period, and by manhood suffrage. It was a small beginning, but who can comprehend or describe the immensity of the outcome?

"They disregarded all authority which they had not themselves instituted or accepted. Religious toleration has been wrought out through infinite human suffering in many countries, but no single community ever made so great a contribution to its ultimate triumph as the Pilgrim State. They had no vision of the ultimate triumph, on a prodigious scale, of the social and governmental principles in support of which they left home and country, and struggled, all their lives, to establish new homes and a new social order, on the edge of an unexplored wilderness, in a severe climate, and in constant apprehension from savage neighbors, domestic enemies, and foreign oppressors.

"They ran visible risks of the most serious character, and made the gravest sacrifices that human beings can make, to their own religious, social and political ideals. All this on hope and faith, without any assurance of success, either for themselves or their descendants. They established a community and a government solidly founded on love of freedom and belief in progress, on civil liberty and religious toleration, on industrial cooperation, and individual honesty and industry, on even-handed justice and a real equality before the laws, on peace and good will, supported by protective force.

"The personal and social virtues of the Mayflower Pilgrims are the surest foundations on which great states may be securely maintained. Therefore they are to be forever remembered with love and honor by the Great Republic which has inherited their ideals."

SENATOR HENRY CABOT LODGE
Ending of oration in Plymouth at the celebration
held on December 21, 1920

'Yet they did not live in vain. They strove to do their best on earth and to make it, so far as they could in their short existence, a better place for their fellow-men. They were not slothful in business, working hard and toiling in their fields and on the stormy northern seas. They sought to give men freedom both in body and mind. They tried to reduce the sum of human misery, the suffering inseparable from human existence. Whatever our faith, whatever our belief in progress, there can be no nobler purposes for man than thus to deal with the only earth he knows and the fragment of time awarded him for his existence here. As we think of them in this the only true way, our reverence and our admiration alike grow ever stronger. We turn to them in gratitude, and we commend what they did and their example to those who come after us. While the great republic is true in heart and deed to the memory of the Pilgrims of Plymouth, it will take no detriment even from the hand of Time."

GOVERNOR (LATER PRESIDENT) COOLIDGE
Tribute to the Pilgrim Fathers delivered at the
celebration held in Plymouth on December 21, 1920

"Three centuries ago today the Pilgrims of the Mayflower made final landing at Plymouth Rock. They came not merely from the shores of the Old World. It will be in vain to search among recorded maps and history for their origin. They sailed up out of the infinite.

"There were among them small trace of the vanities of life. They came undecked with orders of nobility. They were not children of fortune, but of tribulation. Persecution, not preference, brought them hither. But it was a persecution in which they found a stern satisfaction. They cared little for titles, still less for the goods of this earth, but for an idea they would die.

"Measured by the standard of men of their time, they were the humble of the earth. Measured by later accomplishments, they were the mighty. In appearance weak and persecuted they came, rejected, despised, an insignificant band, in reality strong and independent, a mighty host, of whom the world was not worthy, destined to free mankind. No captain ever led his forces to such a conquest. Oblivious to rank, yet men trace to them their lineage as to a royal house.

"Forces not ruled by man had laid their unwilling course. As they landed, a sentinel of Providence, humbler, nearer to nature than themselves, welcomed them in their own tongue. They came seeking an abiding place only on earth, 'but lifted up their eyes to heaven, their dearest country,' says Governor Bradford, 'where God hath prepared for them a city.' On that abiding faith has been reared an empire magnificent beyond their dreams of paradise.

"Amid the solitude they set up heartstone and altar; the home and the church. With arms in their hands they wrung from the soil their bread. With arms they gathered in the congregation to worship Almighty God. But they were armed that, in peace, they might seek divine guidance in righteousness, not that they might prevail by force, but that they might do right though they perished.

"What an increase, material and spiritual, 300 years has brought that little company known to all the earth. No like body ever cast so great an influence on human history. Civilization has made of their landing place a shrine. Unto the Commonwealth of Massachusetts has been intrusted the

186

keeping of that shrine. To her has come the precious heritage. It will be kept as it was created, or it will perish, not with an earthly pride, but with a heavenly vision.

"Plymouth Rock does not mark a beginning or an end. It marks a revelation of that which is without beginning and without end, a purpose, shining through eternity with a resplendent light, undimmed even by the imperfections of men, and a response, an answering purpose, from those who, oblivious, disdainful of all else, sailed hither seeking only for an avenue for the immortal soul." *(See S2).*

On Cole's Hill, in Plymouth, overlooking the spot where the Pilgrims landed, there is a sarcophagus, containing the bones of the first Pilgrim dead. On it is this

INSCRIPTION:

"This monument marks the first burying ground in Plymouth of the Passengers of the Mayflower. Here, under cover of darkness, the fast dwindling Company laid their dead; levelling the earth above them lest the Indians should learn how many were the graves.

"READER, History records no nobler venture for Faith and Freedom than that of this Pilgrim band. In weariness and painfulness, in watchings often, in hunger and cold they laid the foundations of a State wherein every man, through countless ages, should have liberty to worship God in his own way. May their example inspire thee to do thy part in perpetuating and spreading throughout the World the lofty Ideals of our Republic."

REFERENCES

A — Edward Arber, "The Story of the Pilgrim Fathers, 1606-1623," London, 1897. (Includes Mourt's Relation and Winslow's Good Newes.)

AA — Azel Ames, "The Mayflower and Her Log," Boston, 1901.

AD — Charles Francis Adams, "Three Episodes of Massachusetts History," Boston, 1892.

AF — James Truslow Adams, "The Founding of New England," Boston, 1921.

AG — American Genealogist.

AH — Walter E. Allerton, "Isaac Allerton. Allerton Family in the United States, 1585-1885," 1899.

AI — Walter E. Allerton, "A Mayflower Pilgrim and Pioneer of Marblehead," 1899.

AJ — Augustus E. Alden, "John Alden, Pilgrim Alden," 1902.

AK — "Earliest Printed Sources of New England History, 1602-1629," Mass. Hist. Soc. Proc. Vol. IX, pp. 182-192.

AL — Edward M. Bacon, "Historic Pilgrimages in New England."

AM — Americana.

AN — Thomas Prince, "Chronological History of New England in the form of 'Annals,' " 1736.

AO — Lillian Hoag Monk, "Old Pilgrim Days," Los Angeles, 1920.

AP — Mary Alice Tenny, "Selected List of Works in the Public Library of the City of Boston on the Pilgrims," 1920.

AQ — E. S. Hosmer, "Pilgrims in 1620."

AR — Mrs. J. B. Peploe, "Pilgrims of New England."

AS — Robert Ashton, "John Robinson: His Works," Boston, 1851.

AT — C. M. Andrews, "The Fathers of New England," New Haven, 1919.

B — William Bradford, "History of Plymouth Plantation, 1606-1646," Scribner, 1908. (There are many other editions.)

BA — Valerian Paget, "Bradford's History Rendered into Modern English," New York, 1909.*

BB — Letter-Book, Series I, Massachusetts Hist. Soc. Collection, Vols. 3-4, Boston, 1794.

BC — Bradford's Letters to John Winthrop, Series IV, Mass. Hist. Soc. Cols., Vol. 6.

BD — Bradford, "A Dialogue or 3rd Conference," edited by Charles Deane, Boston, 1870.

BE — Thomas Bradford Drew, "The Ancient Estate of Governor William Bradford," 1897.

BG — Walter H. Burgess, "John Robinson, Pastor of the Pilgrim Fathers," 1920.

*See page 196.

BH — G. M. Fessenden, "Bradford Genealogy," New Eng. Hist. & Gen. Reg., Vol. 4, pages 39-50; 233-245.

BI — "Did William Bradford Leave Leyden before the Pilgrims?" Mass. Hist. Soc. Proceedings, Vol. 61, pages 34-40; 55-58.

BJ — Henry M. Dexter, "Elder Brewster's Library," Mass. Hist. Society Paper, Cambridge, 1890.

BK — Charles Edward Banks, "English Ancestry and Homes of the Pilgrim Fathers," Boston, 1929.

BL — Banks' "Index of the Names of Emigrants."

BM — Emma Jones Brewster, "William Brewster, Genealogy of His Descendants," 2 volumes, New York, 1908.

BN — Leonard Bacon, "The Genesis of the New England Churches," New York, 1874.

BO — Hezekiah Butterworth, "Pilot of the Mayflower," New York, 1898.

BR — John Brown, "The Pilgrim Fathers of New England," Third American Edition, 1896.

BT — Charles Knowles Bolton, "The Real Founders of New England," Boston, 1929.

BU — Amory H. Bradford, "The Pilgrims in Old England," 1893.

BV — Francis Baylies, "An Historical Memoir of the Colony of New Plymouth," Boston, 1830.

BW — James Shepard, "William Bradford and his Son Major William Bradford," New Britain, Conn., 1900.

BX — Ashbel Steele, "Life and Times of William Brewster," Philadelphia, 1857.

BY — Mitchell, "History of Bridgewater."

BZ — Amos Otis, "Barnstable Families," Washington, 1885.

C — Henry Cooke, "Memorial of Francis Cooke and His Immediate Descendants," Boston, 1870.

CA — Henry Wyles Cushman, "Genealogy of the Cushmans," 1855.

CB — John Cuckson, "Brief History of the First Church in Plymouth, 1608-1901," Boston, 1902.

CC — Edmund J. Carpenter, "Mayflower Pilgrims. A Story in Popular Manners, 1606-1640," 1918.

CD — Harriet T. Cheyney, "A Peep at the Pilgrims in 1636," Boston, 1850.

CE — Ethel J. R. C. Noyes, "The Women of the Mayflower and Women of Plymouth Colony," 1921.

CF — Freeman, "History of Cape Cod," Boston Vol. I, 1858; Vol. 2, 1862.

CM — Cotton Mather, "Magnalia Christi Americana," London, 1702, Vol. 1 (Edition 1853).

CP — John Masefield, "Chronicles of the Pilgrim Fathers," Everyman's Library, 1910.

CR — "Plymouth Church Records, 1620-1859," Publications of the Colonial Society of Massachusetts, Vol. 22, Boston, 1920.

CS — C. W. Swift, "Cape Cod Library of History and Genealogy."

CT — Helen G. Carlisle, "We Begin."

D — William T. Davis, "Ancient Landmarks of Plymouth," 2nd Edition, Boston, 1899.

DA — Rev. Dr. Samuel M. Worcester, "A Discourse Delivered at Plymouth, Mass., December 22, 1848," Salem, 1849.

DB — Rev. Dr. Abiel Holmes, "Two Discourses on the Completion of the Second Century from the Landing of the Forefathers of New England at Plymouth, 24 December, 1820," Cambridge, 1821.

DC — "An Account of the Pilgrim Celebration at Plymouth, August 1, 1853," Boston, 1853.

DE — S. A. Drake, "On Plymouth Rock," 1897.

DG — Ethan Doty, "Descendants of Edward Doty, an Emigrant on the Mayflower, 1620," 1897.

DH — William T. Davis, "History of the Town of Plymouth," Philadelphia, 1885.

DM — William T. Davis, "Plymouth Memories of an Octogenarian," Plymouth, 1906.

DN — Henry Martyn Dexter and Morton Dexter, "The England and Holland of the Pilgrims," Boston, 1905.

DO — Morton Dexter, "Story of the Pilgrims. Scrooby Club Sketches," Boston, 1894.

DR — Benjamin Drew, "Burial Hill," Plymouth.

DW — George Francis Dow, "Domestic Life in New England in the Seventeenth Century," Topsfield, Mass., 1925.

DY — George Francis Dow, "Every Day Life in the Massachusetts Bay Colony," Boston, 1935.

DZ — Norman H. Dawes, "Titles and Symbols of Prestige in Seventeenth Century New England," The William and Mary Quarterly, January, 1949, Vol. VI, page 69.

E — "The Early Poems of Ralph Waldo Emerson," with an introduction by Nathan Haskell Dole; T. Y. Crowell, New York, 1899.

EA — A. Elkhof, "Three Unknown Documents on the Pilgrim Fathers in Holland," 1920. *

EH — Oliver Wendell Holmes, "Ralph Waldo Emerson," American Men of Letters Series, Cambridge, 1900.

*See page 196.

FA — Francis H. Fuller, "Early New England Fullers," New Eng. Hist. & Gen. Reg., Vol. 55, page 192.

FB — Francis H. Fuller, "John Fuller of Redenhall, England and His Descendants in New England," New York Gen. & Biog. Record, Vol. 33, page 211.

FE — William H. Fuller, "Some Descendants of Edward Fuller of the Mayflower," Fuller Genealogy, Vol. I; 1908.

FH — Thomas Harrington, "Dr. Samuel Fuller of the Mayflower," Baltimore, 1903.

FS — William H. Fuller, "Some Descendants of Samuel Fuller of the Mayflower," Fuller Genealogy, Vol. II; 1910.

FT — William H. Fuller, "Some Descendants of Captain Mathew Fuller," Fuller Genealogy, Vol. III; 1914.

G — John A. Goodwin, "The Pilgrim Republic," Boston, 1888.

GM — G. Mourt—William Bradford and Edward Winslow, "A Relation, or Journall, of the Beginnings and Proceedings of the English Plantation settled at Plimoth, in New England," London, 1622.

GN — "A Brief Relation of the Discovery and Plantation of New England," reprinted in Mass. Hist. Society Coll., XIX, 1-25.

GO — Thomas Robbins, "Historical View of the First Planters," 1815.

GP — Joseph D. Sawyer, "History of the Pilgrims and Puritans," 3 Vols., Century History Co., New York, 1922.

GQ — Alexander Mackennal, "Homes and Haunts of the Pilgrim Fathers," London, 1899, and 1910.

GR — Martin S. Briggs, "Homes of the Pilgrims in England and America, 1620-1685," London and New York, 1932.

GS — J. Ewing Ritchie, "On the Track of the Pilgrim Fathers; or Holidays in Holland," 1866.

GT — Nina M. Tiffany, "Pilgrims and Puritans: Story of the Planting of Plymouth and Boston," Boston, 1896.

GU — William E. Griffis, "Pilgrims in Their Three Homes; England, Holland and America," Riverside Library, 1898.

GV — William E. Griffis, "Young People's History of the Pilgrims," Boston, 1920.

H — Joseph Hunter, "The Founders of New Plymouth," London, 1854.

HA — D. H. Hurd, "History of Plymouth County," 2 Volumes, 1884.

HB — James W. Hawes, "Stephen and Giles Hopkins, Mayflower Passengers and Some of Their Descendants," Cape Cod Library, No. 37.

HC — William Howland, "Pilgrim John Howland, A Mayflower Pilgrim," Pilgrim John Howland Society, 1926.

HD — Charles S. Hanks, "Our Plymouth Forefathers, The Real Founders of Our Republic," Boston, 1897.

HE — Marcus B. Huish, "The American Pilgrim's Way in England," 1907.

HG — "Hochelaga or England in the New World," ed. by Eliot Warburton, London, 1846.

HL — Hildreth, "History of the United States," Vol. I, New York, 1856.

HP — Josiah Paine, "Stephen Hopkins," 1913, Cape Cod.

HS — Leon Clark Hill,* "The Mayflower Planters."

HX — Annie Arnoux Haxtun, "Signers of the Mayflower Compact," New York, 1896-1899.

J — Edward Johnson, "Wonder-Working Providence, 1628-1651," (1910 Edition).

JC — Donald Lines Jacobus, "Index to Genealogical Periodicals."

JM — Professor James R. Jack, "Some Historic Ships."

K — Bradford Kingman, "Epitaphs from Burial Hill," Brookline, 1893.

L — "Leyden Documents Relating to the Pilgrim Fathers," edited by D. Plooy* and J. R. Harris, Leyden, 1920.

LB — J. H. Lefroy, "Memorials of the Bermudas," London, 1877.

LD — Arthur Lord, "Plymouth and the Pilgrims," Boston, 1920.

LH — W. Sears Nickerson, "Land Ho—1620," Houghton, Mifflin Co., 1931.

LI — Charles Thornton Libby, "Mary Chilton's Title to Celebrity," Boston, 1926.

LJ — W. D. Love, "The Fast and Thanksgiving Days of New England," Boston, 1895.

M — Nathaniel Morton, "New England's Memorial," Cambridge, 1669. Editions 1826, 1903, 1937.

MA — Albert C. Addison, "Romantic Story of the Mayflower Pilgrims," Boston, 1911.

MB — Rendel J. Harris, "Finding of the Mayflower," 1920.

MC — Rendel J. Harris, "Last of the Mayflower."

MD — "Mayflower Descendant," published by Massachusetts Society of Mayflower Descendants, 1899 to 1935; 33 volumes.

MH — Massachusetts Historical Society Proceedings, 2nd Series, Vol. 5.

MI — William Alexander McAuslan, "Mayflower Index," 1932.

MJ — M. R. G. Marsden, "Captain Christopher Jones and the Mayflower," English Review, XIX, October, 1904.

MK — Rendel J. Harris, "Return of the Mayflower," 1919.

ML — Jacob B. Moore, "Lives of the Governors of New Plymouth and Massachusetts Bay," Boston, 1851.

*See page 196.

MM — Annie R. Marble, "The Women Who Came in the Mayflower," 1920.

MO — Perry Miller, "Orthodoxy in Massachusetts, 1630-1650," Cambridge, 1933.

MP — Charles Henry Pope, "Pioneers of Massachusetts," Boston, 1900.

MQ — Mayflower Quarterly.

MR — Mourt, "Relation or Journal of the Plantation at Plymouth," with introd. & notes, by Henry Martyn Dexter, Boston, 1865.

MS — Henry Justin Smith, "The Master of the Mayflower," Plimpton Press, 1936.

MT — Albert Matthews, "The Term Pilgrim Fathers," Vol. XVII, Publications of the Colonial Society of Massachusetts.

MW — E. Prescott Sherrill, "The House of Edward Winslow," Plymouth, 1931.

MX — "The Winslow House," pamphlet.

MY — Walter Merriam Pratt, "The Mayflower Society House," Cambridge, 1949.

MZ — Basic Mathews, "Adventures of the Mayflower Pilgrims, The Argonauts of Faith," 1920.*

N — Daniel Neal, "History of the Puritans," London, 1732.

NE — "New England Historical and Genealogical Register."

NG — Savage, "Genealogical Dictionary of New England," 1860.

NL — Thomas W. Mason and B. Nightingale, "New Light on the Pilgrim Story," London, 1920.

NO — Albert J. Nock, "Our Enemy, the State," New York, 1935.

NT — Alden Bradford, "Biographical Notices of Distinguished Men in New England," Boston, 1842.

NU — Frederick A. Noble, "The Pilgrims," Boston, 1907.

NY — "New York Genealogical and Biographical Record."

P — E. B. Patten, "Isaac Allerton," Minneapolis, 1908.

PB — Albert H. Plumb, "William Bradford of Plymouth," Boston, 1920.

PC — D. Plooy,* "The Pilgrim Fathers from a Dutch Point of View," New York, 1932.

PCL — Plymouth Colony Laws; Boston, 1836.

PCR — Plymouth Colony Records, 1633, 1697, 12 volumes, edited by W. B. Shurteff and D. Pulsifer, 1855-1861.

PP — "Phinehas Pratt and Some of His Descendants," Boston, 1897.

PSB — "Plymouth Scrapbook," 1918.

PTR — Plymouth Town Records.

PV — John Pory, "Lost Description of the Plymouth Colony in the Earliest Days of the Pilgrim Fathers," Edited by C. Burrage, 1918.

193

PW — "The Pilgrim Festival Held on Forefather's Day, Plymouth, Dec. 22, 1845"; published by Gen. Soc., M. D.

PX — "Plymouth Plantation," Plymouth, 1948.

R — William S. Russell, "Pilgrim Memorials and Guide to Plymouth," Boston, 1860. Several editions, 1864-1866.

RS — Isaac de Rasieres, Letter, Collections of the New York Historical Society, Second series, II, 351.

S — Reverend Thomas Cruddas Porteus, "Captain Myles Standish: His Lost Lands and Lancashire Connections," London, 1920. (Same in New England Historic and Genealogical Register, Vol. 68.)

SG — Samuel G. Webber, "A Genealogy of the Southworths," Boston, 1905.

SH — J. A. Vinton, "Henry Samson. Genealogical Memoirs of the Sampson Family in America," Boston, 1864.

SN — Henry Hallam Saunderson, "Puritan Principles and American Ideals," The Pilgrim Press, 1930.

SR — G. T. Ridlon, "George Soule. Soule Genealogy."

SV — "Sailor's Narratives of New England Voyages, 1524-1624," Boston, 1905.

SW — Myles Standish, "Myles Standish. Standishes of America," Boston, 1895.

SX — E. J. Huigan, "Graves of Myles Standish and Other Pilgrims," 1914.

SY — Henry Johnson, "The Exploits of Myles Standish," New York, 1897.

SZ — Harry B. Sherman, "Mayflower Pilgrim Declamations," 1948.

T — James Thacher, "History of the Town of Plymouth," Second Edition, Boston, 1835.

TM — Thomas Morton, "New England*Canaan," Amsterdam, 1637; Prince Society reprint, Boston, 1883.

TN — Banks, "Thomas Morton of Merrymount," (Mass. Hist. Soc. Proc., Dec. 1924; Nov. 1925) .

TR — Eliphalet Bradford Terry, "Pilgrim Historical Milestones."

U — Roland G. Usher, "The Pilgrims and Their History," New York, 1918.

W — Edward Winslow, "Good Newes from New England," London, 1624. (MD XXV 151-163) (MD XXVI 11-23, 68-80, 128-138, 150-161) .

WD — Waddington, "Congregational History, 1567-1700," London, 1874.

WE — Weeden, "Economic and Social History of New England," 1620-1789.

*See page 196.

WF — William C. Winslow, "The Pilgrim Fathers in Holland," 1891.

WG — Letter written by Winslow at Barbadoes preserved in Sec. Thurlow's State Papers, III, 250.

WH — Edward Winslow, "Hypocrisie Unmasked," London, 1646.

WI — Three letters from Winslow to Governor Winthrop, one to Commissioners of United Colonies and one to Secretary Thurlow in Hutchinson's Collection of Papers, pp. 60, 110, 153, 228, 268. See also MD XXVI, 97.

WJ — Edward Winslow, "The Glorious Progress of the Gospell amongst the Indians in New England," London, 1649.

WK — Walker, "History of the Congregational Churches," New York, 1894.

WN — Edward Winslow, "New England's Salamander," London, 1647.

WR — Thomas Goddard Wright, "Literary Culture in Early New England," 1620-1730, New Haven, 1920.

WS — Winsor, "The Earliest Printed Sources of New England History," 1602-1629.

WT — Maria W. Bryant, "Edward Winslow of the Mayflower and His Descendants from 1620 to 1865," 1915.

WU — William C. Winslow, "Governor Edward Winslow, His Part and Place in the Plymouth Colony," New York, 1896.

WV — Roebling, "Richard Warren of the Mayflower and Some of His Descendants," Boston, 1901. (See N.E. Vol. 55, pages 70-78; 161-170).

WW — Thomas and Samuel White, "Descendants of William White," 1895.

WX — Daniel Webster, "Discourse Delivered at Plymouth, December 22, 1820." Boston, 1821.

WY — Edward Winslow, "True Reasons for Founding of New Plymouth," London, 1846.

WZ — "Pilgrim Tercentenary Celebration, December 21, 1920," University of Illinois Press, Urbana, 1921.

Y — Alexander Young, "Chronicles of the Pilgrim Fathers of the Colony of Plymouth," Boston, 1841.
      The following are interesting.

YA — Ruth Gardiner Hall, "Descendants of Governor William Bradford," 1951.

ZA — Gleason L. Archer, "Mayflower Heroes," a dramatic presentation of what happened during the first three years of Plymouth Colony, New York, 1935.

ZB — Gleason L. Archer, "With Axe and Musket at Plymouth," a dramatic presentation of the succeeding years to 1630, New York, 1936.

CORRECTIONS

Page 32, line 22 : Insert *known* so line reads: other to receive whatsoever light or truth shall be made *known* to

Page 80, line 21: Insert *crown* before *subsidy*

Page 97, line 30: William White did *not* marry Dr. Samuel Fuller's sister; see *NEHGR* 110:183 and 124:308

Page 102, line 25: Insert *been* so line reads: his mercies endure forever. Yea, let them which have *been* re-

Page 123, line 4: *For* weh *read* w^{ch}

Page 133, line 28: *For* July 23, 1609 *read* June 2, 1609 (see *Mayflower Quarterly*, 35:52, 1969)

Page 135, line 20: *For* was left *read* those left

Page 146, line 12: *For* Swansen *read* Swansea

Page 151, line 1: Insert *future* before *wife*

Page 169, line 4: *For* Chronicales *read* Chronicles

Page 175, line 31: *For* liberay *read* liberty

Page 176, lines 22-24: Quotation should read: "As one small candle may light a thousand, so the light here kindled hath shone to many, yea in some sorte to our whole nation"

Page 188, BA: Title should read: "Bradford's History of the Plymouth Settlement 1608-1650, Rendered into Modern English"

Page 190, EA: *For* Elkhof *read* Eckhof; *for* on *read* Concerning

Page 192, HS: *For* Hill *read* Hills
L: *For* Plooy *read* Plooij

Page 193, MZ: *For* Basic *read* Basil
PC: *For* Plooy *read* Plooij

Page 194, TM: *For* England *read* English

NOTE CONCERNING THE ILLUSTRATIONS

1. Portrait of Governor Edward Winslow is in Pilgrim Hall, Plymouth. It is the only known portrait of any member of the Mayflower company. It was probably painted in London by Robert Walker in 1651.

2. The picture of the Rock shows it as it appears today. There is no known picture of it as it was originally, before any part of it had broken away.   Opposite p. 18

3. The Bradford Bible is one of the most prized possessions of the Pilgrim Society in Pilgrim Hall. It was printed in London in 1594 by Christopher Barker, and was from a translation made by English exiles in Geneva, known as the "Breeches" Bible.   Opposite p. 19

4. Alden house, in Duxbury, is where John and Priscilla Alden passed the last years of their lives and where they died. It was built by their son Jonathan in 1653. It is maintained today as a museum.   Opposite p. 50

5. Howland house, on Sandwish*Street, Plymouth, was built about 1667 and was acquired by Jabez Howland in 1669. John and Elizabeth Howland, parents of Jabez, are said to have lived there for a time. It has been restored so as to appear as it was originally. It is maintained as a museum.   Opposite p. 50

6. The White cabinet is in Pilgrim Hall and tradition ascribes the ownership to William White. Opposite p. 51

7. The Elder Brewster chair is made of ash. It is much more ornate than the Governor Carver chair which has given a name to the type.   Opposite p. 51

8. Scrooby Church was where the Brewsters worshipped in Scrooby, England, until the Elder joined the Separatists.

     Opposite p. 82

*See page 196.

INDEX

BRIDGHAM, Joseph, 86; Mercy, 86; Mercy (Wensley), 86.

BRIGGS, Cyrus, 159; George Russell, 68; Rev. George Ware, 67, 68; Mrs. George W., 68; LeBaron Russell, 49, 68, 104, 118; Rose Thornton, 68.

BRITTERIDGE, RICHARD, 121, 165.

BROOKS, Gov. John, 47; Phillips, 141.

BROWN, 101, 156; Dr. 77; Henry Billings, 141; James, 156; Lydia (Howland), 156; Martha ( ) (Ford), 122; Mary ( ), 122; PETER, 27, 100, 121, 132, 165; Sir Thomas, 100.

BROWNE, John, 121, 122.

BROWNING, Charles, 89.

BRUSTER, William, 95.

BRYANT, William Cullen, 107.

BUCHANAN, James, 13.

BUCKET, Mary, 151.

BURGOYNE, General, 12.

BURKE, 90.

BUTTEN, Robert, 122; William, 88, 122, 131.

CAMEHL, Ada Walker, 48.

CAMPBELL, Prof., 75.

CARLYLE, Thomas, 65, 66, 103.

CARPENTER, Agnes, 131; Alexander, 81, 117, 131; Alice, 81, 117; Edmund J., 168.

CARTER, Robert, 96, 122, 123, 146.

CARTWRIGHT, 94.

CARVER, 48; Catharine (White) (Leggatt), 123, 124; Governor, 78, 96, 98, 108, 117, 147, 156, 161; JOHN, 25, 78, 119, 123, 124, 138, 140, 142, 143, 144, 145, 160, 165; Robert, 78, 123.

CHANDLER, Joseph Everett, 68, 69.

CHARLES I, 95.

CHILTON, Isabel ( ) (Furner), 100; JAMES, 27, 100, 120, 124, 165; John, 100; Lyonel, 100; Mary, 25, 26, 51, 100, 124, 125; Richard or Rychard, 100.

CHOATE, Rufus, 174.

CHURCH, Col. Benjamin, 159.

CHURCHILL, Benjamin, 61; Winston, 142.

CLARK, Faith, 128; Mrs. Hannah, 41; John, 19, 25; Thomas, 19, 41.

CLARKE, Edward, 45; RICHARD, 125, 165.

CLINTON, Sir. Henry, 63.

CLYFTON, Rev. Richard, 77, 115.

COBB, Ephraim, 45; Lemuel, 62.

COCKSHOTT, Winnifred, 168.

COFFIN, Richard, 19.

COKE, 73.

COLBURN, Burnham Standish, 152.

COLKET, Meredith, Jr., XIII.

COLE, James, 56, Joanna, 56. Samuel, 45.

COLLIER, Sarah, 121; William, 121.

CONANT, James Bryant, 107, 118; Rev. Sylvanus, 46.

CONONICUS, 136.

CONNELL, Jerry, 61.

CONWAY, Mrs. Albert, 120.

COOKE, Sir Anthony, 98, 125; FRANCIS, 22, 27, 71, 98, 125, 126, 165; Hester (Mahieux), 98, 125; Jacob, 138; John, 125, 126; John, Jr., 129; Robert, 79; Sarah (Warren), 126.

COOLIDGE, 66; Arthur, 118; Calvin, 7, 185; Charles Allerton, 126.

COOPER, Humility, 127, 153.

COPPIN, Robert, 19, 25.

COPPING, John, 5.

CORLET, Mr., 35.

CORNWALLIS, Lord, 63.

COTTON, 57; Rev. Joshiah, 159; Lucy, 65; Col. Theophilus, 23, 64, 65.

CRACKSTON, Ann, 127; JOHN, 127, 165; John, Jr., 127.

CRANMER, 2.

CRITTENDEN, Lt. John, 111; Maj. Gen. Thomas Leonidas, 111.

CROMWELL, Oliver, 84, 88, 162, 163.

CROSS, Wilbur, 118.

CROSWELL, Andrew, 62.

CROWE, William, 41.

CUFFEE, William, 61.

CURTIS, George William, 179.

CPSIA information can be obtained at www.ICGtesting.com
Printed in the USA
LVOW12s0213300714

396608LV00011B/259/P